Company's Coming®

Everyday Italian

Jean Paré

Sophia De Luca

Il cibo é amore

www.companyscoming.com
visit our website

Front Cover

1. Spaghetti Arcobaleno, page 120

Back Cover

1. Golden Grilled Polenta, page 128
2. Sweet Grilled Fennel, page 128
3. Grilled Italian Veggies, page 131

Everyday Italian

First Printing February 2012

Library and Archives Canada Cataloguing in Publication
Paré, Jean, date
Everyday Italian / Jean Paré.
(Original series)
Includes index.
At head of title: Company's coming.
ISBN 978-1-897477-70-0
1. Cooking, Italian. 2. Cookbooks. I. Title.
II. Series: Paré, Jean, date. Original series.
TX723.P285 2012   641.5945   C2011-906147-3

Published by
Company's Coming Publishing Limited
2311 – 96 Street
Edmonton, Alberta, Canada T6N 1G3
Tel: 780-450-6223   Fax: 780-450-1857
www.companyscoming.com

Company's Coming is a registered trademark owned by Company's Coming Publishing Limited

We acknowledge the financial support of the Government of Canada through the Canada Book Fund for our publishing activities.

Printed in China

We gratefully acknowledge the following suppliers for their generous support of our Test and Photography Kitchens:

Broil King Barbecues
Corelle®
Hamilton Beach® Canada
Lagostina®
Proctor Silex® Canada
Tupperware®

Get more great recipes...FREE!

click

search

print

cook

From apple pie to zucchini bread, we've got you covered. Browse our free online recipes for Guaranteed Great!™ results.

You can also sign up to receive our **FREE online newsletter**. You'll receive exclusive offers, FREE recipes and cooking tips, new title previews, and much more...all delivered to your in-box.

So don't delay, visit our website today!

www.companyscoming.com
visit our website

Company's Coming Cookbooks

Quick & easy recipes; everyday ingredients!

Original Series

- Softcover, 160 pages
- Lay-flat plastic comb binding
- Full-colour photos
- Nutrition information

Original Series

- Softcover, 160 pages
- Lay-flat plastic comb binding
- Full-colour photos
- Nutrition information

Original Series

- Softcover, 160 pages
- Lay-flat plastic comb binding
- Full-colour photos
- Nutrition information

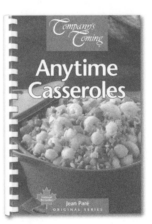

Original Series

- Softcover, 160 pages
- Lay-flat plastic comb binding
- Full-colour photos
- Nutrition information

For a complete listing of our cookbooks, visit our website:
www.companyscoming.com

Table of Contents

Appetizers

Salads & Soups

Beef

Fish & Seafood

Vegetarian

Pasta & Noodles

Sides

Sweets

The Company's Coming Story

Jean Paré (pronounced "jeen PAIR-ee") grew up understanding that the combination of family, friends and home cooking is the best recipe for a good life. From her mother, she learned to appreciate good cooking, while her father praised even her earliest attempts in the kitchen. When Jean left home, she took with her a love of cooking, many family recipes and an intriguing desire to read cookbooks as if they were novels!

"Never share a recipe you wouldn't use yourself."

When her four children had all reached school age, Jean volunteered to cater the 50th anniversary celebration of the Vermilion School of Agriculture, now Lakeland College, in Alberta, Canada. Working out of her home, Jean prepared a dinner for more than 1,000 people, launching a flourishing catering operation that continued for over 18 years. During that time, she had countless opportunities to test new ideas with immediate feedback—resulting in empty plates and contented customers! Whether preparing cocktail sandwiches for a house party or serving a hot meal for 1,500 people, Jean Paré earned a reputation for great food, courteous service and reasonable prices.

As requests for her recipes increased, Jean was often asked the question, "Why don't you write a cookbook?" Jean responded by teaming up with her son, Grant Lovig, in the fall of 1980 to form Company's Coming Publishing Limited. The publication of *150 Delicious Squares* on April 14, 1981 marked the debut of what would soon become one of the world's most popular cookbook series.

The company has grown since those early days when Jean worked from a spare bedroom in her home. Nowadays every Company's Coming recipe is *kitchen-tested* before it is approved for publication.

Company's Coming cookbooks are distributed in Canada, the United States, Australia and other world markets. Bestsellers many times over in English, Company's Coming cookbooks have also been published in French and Spanish.

Familiar and trusted in home kitchens around the world, Company's Coming cookbooks are offered in a variety of formats. Highly regarded as kitchen workbooks, the softcover Original Series, with its lay-flat plastic comb binding, is still a favourite among readers.

Jean Paré's approach to cooking has always called for *quick and easy recipes* using *everyday ingredients*. That view has served her well. The recipient of many awards, including the Queen Elizabeth Golden Jubilee Medal, Jean was appointed Member of the Order of Canada, her country's highest lifetime achievement honour.

Jean continues to share what she calls The Golden Rule of Cooking: *Never share a recipe you wouldn't use yourself*. It's an approach that has worked—*millions of times over!*

Foreword

La vita e bella! Italy has an undeniable sense of beauty and romance: the countryside, the artwork, the language and especially the food!

In *Everyday Italian* we try to capture the intrigue and mystery of all things Italian—in a way that's simple and can be achieved everyday. You'll discover that Italian cooking is much more than just pizza and pasta—but rest assured, we couldn't make an Italian cookbook without including those as well!

One of the best parts of Italian cooking is how easy it is to prepare. With a few simple ingredients, you can make a tasty, nutritious meal in no time. Plus, the availability of diverse ingredients at supermarkets and specialty Italian stores has made it easier than ever to put delicious Italian fare on the table at home. To make it even easier, we've included a list of essential Italian ingredients to help you stock your pantry for last-minute meals.

You'll find a wide range of options in *Everyday Italian*, from breakfasts and brunches to main courses, sides, soups, salads and desserts. We've included many classic Italian recipes like Pasta e Fagioli, Pizza Margherita and Spaghetti Bolognese.

You'll also find many recipes that put a new twist on tradition, such as our Sage Chicken Ravioli that uses wonton wrappers in place of homemade pasta dough and our Veggie Ball Spaghetti that provides a vegetarian version of the classic spaghetti and meatballs. You'll even find a section of delectable sweets, including Chocolate Fig Biscotti and Sweet Basil Panna Cotta.

What are you waiting for? Everyone in the family will love these Italian recipes, any day of the week. It's easy to begin your tour of *la cucina italiana* with *Everyday Italian!*

Jean Paré

Nutrition Information Guidelines

Each recipe is analyzed using the most current versions of the Canadian Nutrient File from Health Canada, and the United States Department of Agriculture (USDA) Nutrient Database for Standard Reference.

- If more than one ingredient is listed (such as "butter or hard margarine"), or if a range is given (1 – 2 tsp., 5 – 10 mL), only the first ingredient or first amount is analyzed.
- For meat, poultry and fish, the recommended serving size per person is 4 oz. (113 g) uncooked weight (without bone), which is 2 – 3 oz. (57 – 85 g) cooked weight (without bone)—approximately the size of a deck of playing cards.
- Milk used is 1% M.F. (milk fat), unless otherwise stated.
- Cooking oil used is canola oil, unless otherwise stated.
- Ingredients indicating "sprinkle," "optional" or "for garnish" are not included in the nutrition information.
- The fat in recipes and combination foods can vary greatly depending upon the sources and types of fats used in each specific ingredient. For these reasons, the amount of saturated, monounsaturated and polyunsaturated fats may not add up to the total fat content.

Italian Understood

Most people are already somewhat familiar with Italian food—it's a very popular style of regional cooking. However, there is much more to learn about the regions of Italy and the flavours associated with each of them, and about Italian culinary traditions.

A Regional Tour

Italy is made up of 20 distinct regions, but the cuisine styles can be loosely grouped into four main regions: northern Italy, central Italy, southern Italy and Sicily.

Northern Italy: Home to the cities of Venice, Torino and Milan, northern Italy draws its culinary inspirations from the neighbouring countries of France, Germany and Austria. Meals in the north of Italy contain more meat, especially beef, veal and pork. Butter is more commonly used than olive oil here. Tomatoes are not as prevalent in northern Italian dishes as they are in the south. Stuffed pastas are popular and starchy dishes like polenta and risotto hail from this region.

Central Italy: Rome is located in the central region of Italy, which is known for its culinary simplicity. Cheeses, pasta, breads, cured meats, legumes, vegetables and wine are staples in meals of this region. Many well-known Italian dishes, such as Florentine steak and panforte, can be traced back to central Italy's Tuscany region.

Southern Italy: The food of the southern region makes up a large part of what North Americans consider Italian food—think lasagna, pizza and eggplant parmigiana. Olive oil is a very important ingredient here. Vegetables like tomatoes grow well in the warm climate, and so are fixtures in the southern diet. This region is home to Naples, with many dishes of the area referred to as "Neapolitan."

Sicily: Although technically a part of southern Italy, this small island off the coast of mainland Italy has its own strong culinary history, incorporating influences from many neighbouring regions such as North Africa, Greece and Spain. Pasta was first made in Siciliy. Sweets are common here, with dried fruits, honey and ricotta cheese appearing in many Sicilian-style desserts and treats. Seafood is another important aspect of this region's cookery.

Meal Structure

The typical Italian meal follows a different structure than most North Americans are used to. Meals often contain three or four courses, with pasta often served separately from the main course.

Antipasto (also called *antipasti*) literally means "before the meal" and can be a mix of hot or cold appetizers. Often it comes in the form of an antipasti platter of cold meats and vegetables. Following the antipasto is the first course or *primo*, which is often a pasta dish but can also be polenta, risotto or soup depending on the region of Italy you're in. Next comes the main course or *secondo*, which is often a meat or seafood dish that is accompanied by a side dish or *contorno* of a salad or vegetables. Some sweets or *dolce* may come at the end of the meal, perhaps served with a cup of coffee (*caffè*).

The number of courses and variety of dishes served means that some Italian meals, especially those at large occasions and festive celebrations, take a number of hours to conclude. Even typical meals consist of more than one course, which allows family and friends time to visit with one another. Italians refuse to sacrifice the practice of savouring their food, even in their busy, modern lives.

Essential Italian Ingredients

To easily put together meals with Italian flavours, we suggest keeping the following pantry ingredients on hand.

Cans, Jars and Bottles
Artichoke hearts
  Canned
  Marinated
Basil pesto
Beans
  White kidney beans
  Chickpeas (garbanzo beans)
  Romano beans
Capers
Olive (or cooking) oil
Olives
  Black
  Green
Pasta sauces
  Alfredo
  Tomato
Tomatoes
  Sun-dried tomatoes in oil
  Tomato paste

Cheeses
Asiago
Italian cheese blend
Mozzarella
Fresh Parmesan

Dried Goods
Arborio rice
Dried porcini mushrooms
Pasta
  A variety of short and long
Pine nuts
Yellow cornmeal

Herbs and Seasonings
Basil
Dried crushed chilies
Garlic powder
Italian seasoning
Oregano
Rosemary

Grilled Caponata

This classic Sicilian dish is commonly served as an appetizer, condiment or side dish and is known for its intense olive flavour. Serve caponata (pronounced kap-oh-NAH-tah) with crostini or sliced ciabatta loaf.

Olive oil	3 tbsp.	50 mL
Garlic clove, minced (or 1/4 tsp., 1 mL, powder)	1	1
Medium Roma (plum) tomatoes, halved lengthwise	5	5
Medium fennel bulb (white part only), cut crosswise into 1/2 inch (12 mm) slices	1	1
Medium onion, cut crosswise into 1/2 inch (12 mm) slices	1	1
Small eggplant (with peel), cut lengthwise into 1/4 inch (6 mm) slices	1	1
Chopped pimiento-stuffed olives	1/2 cup	125 mL
Pine nuts, toasted (see Tip, page 46)	1/4 cup	60 mL
Tomato sauce	1/4 cup	60 mL
Chopped fresh parsley	2 tbsp.	30 mL
Red wine vinegar	2 tbsp.	30 mL
Brown sugar, packed	1 tsp.	5 mL
Dried oregano	1/4 tsp.	1 mL
Salt	3/4 tsp.	4 mL
Pepper	1/4 tsp.	1 mL

Combine olive oil and garlic in small cup.

Brush next 4 ingredients with olive oil mixture. Preheat gas barbecue to medium-high. Arrange vegetables on greased grill. Close lid. Cook for about 5 minutes per side until grill marks appear and vegetables are softened. Transfer to cutting board. Let stand until cool enough to handle. Chop finely. Transfer to large bowl.

Combine remaining 9 ingredients in small bowl. Add to vegetable mixture. Stir. Makes about 4 1/2 cups (1.1 L).

1/4 cup (60 mL): 60 Calories; 4.5 g Total Fat (2.5 g Mono, 1.0 g Poly, 0.5 g Sat); 0 mg Cholesterol; 5 g Carbohydrate; 2 g Fibre; trace Protein; 190 mg Sodium

Lemon Garlic Calamari

Deep-fried calamari can be so heavy. This lighter pan-fried version allows you to enjoy the mild flavour of squid along with lovely lemon and garlic accents. Just be careful not to overcook, because overcooking gives calamari a chewy texture.

Olive oil	2 tbsp.	30 mL
Garlic cloves, minced	2	2
Dried crushed chilies	1/8 tsp.	0.5 mL
Small squid tubes, cut into 1/2 inch (12 mm) rings (see Tip, below)	1 lb.	454 g
Lemon juice	1 tbsp.	15 mL
Chopped fresh oregano	1/2 tsp.	2 mL
Salt	1/2 tsp.	2 mL
Pepper	1/8 tsp.	0.5 mL

Heat olive oil in medium frying pan on medium. Add garlic and chilies. Heat and stir for about 1 minute until fragrant.

Add squid. Cook for about 4 minutes, stirring constantly, until squid is opaque and just cooked through. Remove from heat.

Add remaining 4 ingredients. Toss until coated. Makes about 1 3/4 cups (425 mL).

1/4 cup (60 mL): 100 Calories; 4.5 g Total Fat (3.0 g Mono, 1.0 g Poly, 1.0 g Sat); 150 mg Cholesterol; 3 g Carbohydrate; 0 g Fibre; 10 g Protein; 160 mg Sodium

 tip Look for small (young) squid tubes that are not too thick, because they will be more tender than larger, thicker squid tubes when cooked.

Quick Pizza Dip

Enjoy pizza flavours in a simple, crowd-pleasing dip that heats up quickly in the microwave. Serve with breadsticks, baguette slices or tortilla chips.

Block cream cheese, softened	4 oz.	125 g
Sour cream	1/2 cup	125 mL
Pizza sauce	1/2 cup	125 mL
Basil pesto	1 tsp.	5 mL
Diced seeded tomato	1/2 cup	125 mL
Finely chopped yellow pepper	1/4 cup	60 mL
Thinly sliced deli pepperoni sticks	1/4 cup	60 mL
Sliced green onion	2 tbsp.	30 mL
Grated mozzarella cheese	1 cup	250 mL

Beat cream cheese and sour cream in small bowl until smooth. Spread in ungreased 9 inch (23 cm) glass pie plate.

Combine pizza sauce and pesto in separate small bowl. Spread over cream cheese mixture, almost to edge.

Scatter remaining 5 ingredients, in order given, over pizza sauce mixture. Microwave, uncovered, on high (100%) for about 2 minutes until mozzarella cheese is melted (see Tip, page 133). Let stand for 1 minute. Makes about 3 cups (750 mL).

1/4 cup (60 mL): 100 Calories; 8.0 g Total Fat (1.5 g Mono, 0 g Poly, 4.5 g Sat); 25 mg Cholesterol; 2 g Carbohydrate; 0 g Fibre; 4 g Protein; 210 mg Sodium

Spicy Sausage Starter

Some like it hot, and if you do, this recipe will be love at first bite. Hot Italian sausage adds a spicy punch to this otherwise unassuming topping for sliced baguette.

Cooking oil	1 tsp.	5 mL
Hot Italian sausage	1 lb.	454 g
Sliced red pepper	1 1/2 cups	375 mL
Sliced onion	1 cup	250 mL
Garlic cloves, sliced	2	2

(continued on next page)

Chopped fresh oregano (or 1/2 tsp., 2 mL, dried)	2 tsp.	10 mL
Baguette bread loaf, sliced	1	1

Heat cooking oil in large frying pan on medium. Add sausage. Cook for about 10 minutes, turning occasionally, until browned. Remove to cutting board. Cut into 1/2 inch (12 mm) thick slices.

Add next 3 ingredients and sausage slices to same frying pan. Cook for about 8 minutes, stirring occasionally, until onion is softened and sausage is no longer pink.

Add oregano. Stir. Serve with bread slices. Serves 8.

1 serving: 330 Calories; 19.0 g Total Fat (1.0 g Mono, 0.5 g Poly, 6.0 g Sat); 45 mg Cholesterol; 26 g Carbohydrate; 2 g Fibre; 13 g Protein; 790 mg Sodium

---

Artichoke Salami Pizzettes

Full-sized pizzas are so old fashioned. These cute little mini pizzas make a bold flavour statement—and a chic addition to any appetizer tray.

Basil pesto	1/4 cup	60 mL
Unbaked pizza crust (12 inch, 30 cm, diameter)	1	1
Grated Italian cheese blend	1/2 cup	125 mL
Finely chopped marinated artichoke hearts	1/4 cup	60 mL
Finely chopped salami (such as Genoa)	1/4 cup	60 mL
Finely chopped sun-dried tomatoes in oil	1/4 cup	60 mL

Spread pesto on pizza crust. Cut out circles with 2 inch (5 cm) round cookie cutter. Arrange on greased baking sheet with sides. Discard remaining pizza crust scraps.

Combine remaining 4 ingredients in small bowl. Spoon about 2 tsp. (10 mL) onto pizza crust rounds. Bake in 400°F (205°C) oven for about 12 minutes until cheese is melted and golden. Makes about 22 pizzettes.

1 pizzette: 60 Calories; 3 g Total Fat (0 g Mono, 0 g Poly, 1.0 g Sat); trace Cholesterol; 6 g Carbohydrate; trace Fibre; 2 g Protein; 170 mg Sodium

Antipasti Platter

Antipasti, *the plural form of* antipasto, *is an assortment of appetizers. The term literally means "before the meal" in Italian. This selection of meats, cheeses and vegetables is the perfect start to a true Italian meal. Use regular breadsticks if you can't find grissini.*

Basil pesto	2 tbsp.	30 mL
Olive oil	1 tbsp.	15 mL
Salt	1/8 tsp.	0.5 mL
Pepper	1/8 tsp.	0.5 mL
Cocktail bocconcini (fresh mozzarella), about 3/4 inch (2 cm) diameter	16	16
Prosciutto (or deli) ham slices (about 8 oz., 225 g)	16	16
Grissini (Italian breadsticks)	16	16
Assorted olives	1 cup	250 mL
Cherry (or grape) tomatoes	1 cup	250 mL
Sliced English cucumber (with peel)	1 cup	250 mL
Large fennel bulb (white part only), cut into thin wedges	1	1
Large yellow pepper, cut into thin strips	1	1
Radishes, halved	6	6

Combine first 4 ingredients in medium bowl. Add bocconcini. Stir until coated. Chill, covered, for at least 1 hour to blend flavours.

Wrap 1 slice of prosciutto around 1 end of each grissini.

Arrange remaining 6 ingredients, bocconcini and prosciutto-wrapped grissini on large serving platter. Serves 8.

1 serving: 230 Calories; 15.0 g Total Fat (4.5 g Mono, 0.5 g Poly, 5.0 g Sat); 40 mg Cholesterol; 11 g Carbohydrate; 3 g Fibre; 15 g Protein; 1060 mg Sodium

Pictured on page 17.

Prosciutto Polenta Bites

Though polenta may not come to mind when you think of appetizers, this unique recipe puts it to clever use. Little hand-held squares of polenta pack a salty prosciutto accent. Use spinach in place of arugula if you prefer.

Prepared chicken broth	2 cups	500 mL
Half-and-half cream	1 cup	250 mL
Butter (or hard margarine)	1 tbsp.	15 mL
Granulated sugar	1/2 tsp.	2 mL
Pepper	1/2 tsp.	2 mL
Yellow cornmeal	1 cup	250 mL
Finely chopped arugula, lightly packed	1 cup	250 mL
Finely chopped prosciutto (or deli) ham	1/4 cup	60 mL
Grated Parmesan cheese	1/4 cup	60 mL
Lemon juice	1 tbsp.	15 mL
Butter (or hard margarine), melted	1 tsp.	5 mL

Combine first 5 ingredients in large saucepan. Bring to a boil. Reduce heat to medium.

Slowly add cornmeal, stirring constantly. Heat and stir for about 8 minutes until mixture thickens and pulls away from side of pan.

Stir in next 4 ingredients. Remove from heat. Spread evenly in greased foil-lined 9 x 9 inch (23 x 23 cm) pan. Let stand for about 30 minutes until firm (see Note). Remove to cutting board.

Brush top with melted butter. Cut into 49 squares. Arrange on greased baking sheet. Broil on top rack in oven for about 7 minutes until golden and heated through. Makes 49 polenta bites.

1 polenta bite: 25 Calories; 1.0 g Total Fat (0 g Mono, 0 g Poly, 0.5 g Sat); trace Cholesterol; 3 g Carbohydrate; trace Fibre; trace Protein; 55 mg Sodium

Pictured on page 18.

Note: You can prepare the polenta bites up to this point up to 1 day in advance. Chill, covered, until ready to bake.

Sun-Dried Tomato Bruschetta

The addition of sun-dried tomato makes ordinary bruschetta extraordinary.
There's no shortage of flavour intensity here—garlic, green onion, fresh basil
and two types of tomato pack a lot of punch.

Chopped seeded Roma (plum) tomato	2 cups	500 mL
Sun-dried tomatoes in oil, chopped	1/2 cup	125 mL
Finely shredded basil	1/4 cup	60 mL
Sliced green onion	2 tbsp.	30 mL
Oil from sun-dried tomatoes	1 tbsp.	15 mL
Red wine vinegar	2 tsp.	10 mL
Garlic clove, minced (or 1/4 tsp., 1 mL, powder)	1	1
Salt, sprinkle		
Pepper, sprinkle		
Baguette bread slices (1/2 inch, 12 mm, thick)	32	32

Combine first 9 ingredients in medium bowl. Let stand for 30 minutes to blend flavours.

Arrange bread slices on ungreased baking sheet. Broil on top rack in oven for about 1 minute per side until golden. Spoon tomato mixture over top. Serve immediately. Makes 32 bruschetta.

1 bruschetta: 35 Calories; 1.0 g Total Fat (0.5 g Mono, 0 g Poly, 0 g Sat); 0 mg Cholesterol;
5 g Carbohydrate; trace Fibre; trace Protein; 55 mg Sodium

Pictured on page 18.

Antipasti Platter, page 14

Props: Cherison Enterprises

Appetizers

Sweet Pepper Crostini

Easy and versatile recipes are the best friend of any cook. This recipe comes together quickly and can be served hot or cold. Goat cheese and fresh basil add a special touch.

Olive oil	1 tbsp.	15 mL
Thinly sliced red pepper	1 1/2 cups	375 mL
Thinly sliced yellow pepper	1 1/2 cups	375 mL
Garlic cloves, thinly sliced	3	3
Salt, sprinkle		
Pepper, sprinkle		
Whole-wheat baguette bread slices, cut diagonally, 1/4 inch (6 mm) thick	18	18
Goat (chèvre) cheese, cut up	3 oz.	85 g
Finely shredded basil	2 tbsp.	30 mL

Heat olive oil in large frying pan on medium. Add next 5 ingredients. Cook for about 15 minutes, stirring occasionally, until peppers are softened.

Arrange bread slices on ungreased baking sheet. Broil on top rack in oven for about 1 minute per side until golden. Spoon pepper mixture over top.

Sprinkle with goat cheese and basil. Makes 18 crostini.

1 crostini: 50 Calories; 2.5 g Total Fat (1.0 g Mono, 0 g Poly, 1.0 g Sat); trace Cholesterol; 6 g Carbohydrate; trace Fibre; 2 g Protein; 50 mg Sodium

Pictured at left.

1. Sun-Dried Tomato Bruschetta, page 16
2. Prosciutto Polenta Bites, page 15
3. Sweet Pepper Crostini, above

Tuna Salad Sandwiches

If your tuna sandwiches have become rather dull, add an Italian twist to bring them back to life. Fresh basil, tomato slices, garlic and capers add interest to these impressive open-faced sandwiches.

Baguette bread loaf	1	1
Olive oil	1 tbsp.	15 mL
Garlic clove, minced (or 1/4 tsp., 1 mL, powder)	1	1
Cans of flaked white tuna in water, drained (6 oz., 170 g, each)	2	2
Chopped fresh basil	2 tbsp.	30 mL
Chopped fresh parsley	2 tbsp.	30 mL
Finely chopped red onion	2 tbsp.	30 mL
Olive oil	2 tbsp.	30 mL
Capers, chopped	1 tbsp.	15 mL
Lemon juice	1 tbsp.	15 mL
Salt	1/8 tsp.	0.5 mL
Pepper	1/4 tsp.	1 mL
Roma (plum) tomato slices	16	16

Cut baguette in half crosswise. Cut each piece in half lengthwise.

Combine first amount of olive oil and garlic in small bowl. Brush on cut sides of bread pieces. Place on ungreased baking sheet with sides. Broil on top rack in oven for 1 to 2 minutes until golden. Let stand until cool.

Combine next 9 ingredients in medium bowl. Spoon over bread pieces.

Arrange tomato slices on top. Makes 4 open-faced sandwiches.

1 open-faced sandwich: 320 Calories; 13.0 g Total Fat (8.0 g Mono, 1.5 g Poly, 2.5 g Sat); 20 mg Cholesterol; 35 g Carbohydrate; 3 g Fibre; 20 g Protein; 680 mg Sodium

Breakfast Pizza

This unique recipe will reunite you with the pleasures of having a slice of pizza for breakfast. Who would have guessed that all your breakfast staples could be used as pizza toppings?

Tube of refrigerator pizza dough	14 oz.	391 g
Frozen hash brown potatoes	3/4 cup	175 mL
Chopped seeded tomato	1/2 cup	125 mL
Bacon slices, cooked crisp and crumbled	4	4
Finely chopped red onion	2 tbsp.	30 mL
Large eggs	4	4
Milk	3 tbsp.	50 mL
Dried oregano	1/4 tsp.	1 mL
Pepper	1/8 tsp.	0.5 mL
Grated Italian cheese blend	1 1/2 cups	375 mL

Gently press dough in bottom and 1 inch (2.5 cm) up sides of greased 9 x 13 inch (23 x 33 cm) pan.

Scatter next 4 ingredients, in order given, over dough.

Whisk next 4 ingredients in small bowl. Pour over top.

Sprinkle with cheese. Bake in 400°F (205°C) oven for about 20 minutes until egg mixture is set and crust is golden brown. Let stand for 5 minutes. Cuts into 8 pieces.

1 piece: 280 Calories; 11.0 g Total Fat (2.5 g Mono, 0.5 g Poly, 4.5 g Sat); 90 mg Cholesterol; 30 g Carbohydrate; trace Fibre; 14 g Protein; 610 mg Sodium

There is much debate about the origins of the word *pizza*. Some say it came from the Latin *pinsa*, while others insist that the Middle Eastern *pita* is the source. These terms both essentially mean flatbread, which makes sense since pizza is generally served on a flat crust! Today, Italians eat about 7 million pizzas a day.

Breakfast Berry Compote

Balsamic vinegar heightens the berry flavours in this tart topping for pancakes or hot cereal. Also good served chilled over rolls or bread.

Frozen mixed berries, thawed	1 cup	250 mL
Sliced fresh strawberries	1 cup	250 mL
Mixed fruit (or berry) jam	1/2 cup	125 mL
Balsamic vinegar	2 tbsp.	30 mL
Ground cinnamon	1/4 tsp.	1 mL

Combine all 5 ingredients in medium saucepan. Cook, uncovered, on medium for about 5 minutes, stirring occasionally, until mixture comes to a boil. Makes about 2 cups (500 mL).

1/4 cup (60 mL): 80 Calories; 0 g Total Fat (0 g Mono, 0 g Poly, 0 g Sat); 0 mg Cholesterol; 21 g Carbohydrate; 1 g Fibre; 0 g Protein; 0 mg Sodium

Vegetable Polenta Stacks

These stacks are a great lunch option. Use remaining polenta in Saucy Polenta Bake, page 104, or Golden Grilled Polenta, page 128.

Balsamic vinegar	1 tbsp.	15 mL
Olive oil	1 tbsp.	15 mL
Dijon mustard	2 tsp.	10 mL
Dried thyme	1/2 tsp.	2 mL
Pepper	1/4 tsp.	1 mL
Sliced portobello mushrooms	2 cups	500 mL
Sliced small zucchini (with peel)	2 cups	500 mL
Sliced red pepper	1 cup	250 mL
Coarsely crushed seasoned croutons	1/2 cup	125 mL
Polenta roll (2.2 lbs., 1 kg), cut into 8 slices	1/2	1/2
Coarsely crushed seasoned croutons	1/2 cup	125 mL
Olive oil	1 tbsp.	15 mL

Combine first 5 ingredients in large bowl.

Add next 4 ingredients. Toss.

(continued on next page)

Arrange 4 polenta slices in greased 9 x 9 inch (23 x 23 cm) pan. Spoon vegetable mixture over top. Cover with remaining polenta slices.

Combine second amount of croutons and olive oil in small bowl. Sprinkle over top. Cook, covered, in 375°F (190°C) oven for about 20 minutes until vegetables are almost tender. Remove cover. Cook for another 15 minutes until golden. Makes 4 stacks.

1 stack: 240 Calories; 9.0 g Total Fat (6.0 g Mono, 1.0 g Poly, 1.5 g Sat); 0 mg Cholesterol; 35 g Carbohydrate; 5 g Fibre; 7 g Protein; 560 mg Sodium

Eggplant Frittata

Frittatas are the Italian version of omelettes—except they aren't folded and they generally finish cooking under a broiler. This version includes plenty of Italian flavours from eggplant, red pepper and seasonings.

Cooking oil	2 tsp.	10 mL
Finely chopped peeled eggplant	1 1/2 cups	375 mL
Dried oregano	1/4 tsp.	1 mL
Large eggs	8	8
Finely chopped roasted red peppers	1/4 cup	60 mL
Sliced green onion	2 tbsp.	30 mL
Garlic powder	1/4 tsp.	1 mL
Salt	1/2 tsp.	2 mL
Pepper	1/4 tsp.	1 mL

Heat cooking oil in large non-stick frying pan on medium. Add eggplant and oregano. Cook for about 4 minutes, stirring occasionally, until eggplant is softened.

Whisk remaining 6 ingredients in medium bowl. Pour over eggplant mixture. Reduce heat to medium-low. Cook, covered, for about 8 minutes until bottom is golden and top is almost set. Broil on centre rack in oven for about 3 minutes until set (see Tip, below). Cuts into 6 wedges.

1 wedge: 90 Calories; 7.0 g Total Fat (3.0 g Mono, 1.0 g Poly, 1.5 g Sat); 185 mg Cholesterol; 2 g Carbohydrate; trace Fibre; 6 g Protein; 310 mg Sodium

 tip When baking or broiling food in a frying pan with a handle that isn't ovenproof, wrap the handle in foil and keep it to the front of the oven, away from the element.

Prosciutto Pepper Quesadillas

Tasty Italian flavours in a decidedly Mexican format.
This is fusion cuisine at its finest!

Slivered red pepper	1 cup	250 mL
Chopped arugula, lightly packed	1/2 cup	125 mL
Chopped prosciutto (or deli) ham	1/4 cup	60 mL
Grated mozzarella cheese	1 cup	250 mL
Flour tortillas (9 inch, 23 cm, diameter)	2	2
Cooking oil	1/2 tsp.	2 mL

Combine first 3 ingredients in small bowl.

Sprinkle 1/4 cup (60 mL) cheese over half of each tortilla. Spoon red pepper mixture over cheese. Sprinkle remaining cheese over top. Fold tortillas in half to cover filling. Press down lightly.

Brush both sides of quesadillas with cooking oil. Heat large frying pan on medium. Add quesadillas. Cook for about 4 minutes until bottom is golden. Turn. Cook for about 2 minutes until bottom is golden and cheese is melted. Cuts into 4 wedges each, for a total of 8 wedges.

1 wedge: 110 Calories; 6.0 g Total Fat (1.5 g Mono, 0 g Poly, 2.5 g Sat); 15 mg Cholesterol; 8 g Carbohydrate; trace Fibre; 8 g Protein; 460 mg Sodium

Panini Pronto

Hardly got a minute to spare, but in dire need of a satisfying lunch?
This recipe uses a simple grilled-cheese method for a panini that's sure
to fill the hunger gap.

Sun-dried tomato pesto	4 tsp.	20 mL
Sourdough bread slices (1/2 inch, 12 mm, thick)	4	4
Provolone cheese slices (about 3 oz., 85 g)	4	4
Deli ham slices (about 3 oz., 85 g)	4	4
Large basil leaves	4	4
Butter (or hard margarine), softened	4 tsp.	20 mL

(continued on next page)

Spread pesto over bread slices.

Layer cheese, ham and basil over pesto on 2 bread slices. Cover with remaining bread slices, pesto-side down.

Preheat large frying pan on medium. Spread butter on outsides of sandwiches. Cook sandwiches for about 3 minutes per side, pressing down occasionally with spatula until bread is golden and cheese is melted. Makes 2 panini.

1 panini: 679 Calories; 26.0 g Total Fat (2.0 g Mono, 0 g Poly, 14.0 g Sat); 75 mg Cholesterol; 74 g Carbohydrate; 4 g Fibre; 33 g Protein; 1560 mg Sodium

Breakfast Tiramisu

If you'd rather skip the meal and go straight to dessert, this is just the recipe for you. Begin your day with the flavours of a very popular Italian dessert—with a convenient dose of coffee built right in.

Hot strong prepared coffee	1/2 cup	125 mL
Brown sugar, packed	2 tbsp.	30 mL
Raisin bread slices, toasted and crusts removed	8	8
Mascarpone (or cream) cheese	1 1/2 cups	375 mL
Vanilla yogurt	1 1/2 cups	375 mL
Vanilla extract	1/2 tsp.	2 mL
Cocoa, sifted if lumpy	1 tbsp.	15 mL

Stir coffee and brown sugar in small cup until brown sugar is dissolved. Let stand until cool.

Arrange 4 toast slices in single layer in 8 x 8 inch (20 x 20 cm) baking dish, trimming to fit if necessary. Brush with half of coffee mixture.

Combine next 3 ingredients in medium bowl. Spread half over toast slices in pan. Repeat with remaining toast slices, coffee mixture and cheese mixture. Chill, covered, for at least 6 hours or overnight.

Sprinkle with cocoa. Cuts into 9 pieces.

1 piece: 240 Calories; 15.0 g Total Fat (1.5 g Mono, 0 g Poly, 9.0 g Sat); 45 mg Cholesterol; 21 g Carbohydrate; 1 g Fibre; 6 g Protein; 200 mg Sodium

Pictured on page 35.

Muffuletta Strata

*The muffuletta (pronounced mooh-fuh-LEHT-tuh) sandwich may originate
from New Orleans, though it's certainly packed with popular Italian flavours.
This tasty strata version makes the perfect brunch.*

French bread slices (1/2 inch, 12 mm, thick)	12	12
Grated provolone cheese	1 cup	250 mL
Chopped deli ham	3/4 cup	175 mL
Chopped Genoa salami slices	3/4 cup	175 mL
Large eggs	6	6
Milk	1 cup	250 mL
Dried oregano	1 tsp.	5 mL
Garlic powder	1/4 tsp.	1 mL
Pepper	1/4 tsp.	1 mL
Chopped seeded tomato	1/2 cup	125 mL
Jar of marinated artichoke hearts, drained and chopped	6 oz.	170 mL
Sliced kalamata olives	1/4 cup	60 mL
Sliced pimiento-stuffed olives	1/4 cup	60 mL
Capers (optional)	1 tbsp.	15 mL

Arrange bread slices, slightly overlapping, in greased 9 x 13 inch
(23 x 33 cm) pan.

Scatter next 3 ingredients over bread slices.

Whisk next 5 ingredients in medium bowl. Pour over top. Chill, covered, for
at least 6 hours or overnight. Bake, uncovered, in 350°F (175°C) oven for
about 30 minutes until puffed and golden.

Scatter remaining 5 ingredients over top. Serves 6.

*1 serving: 320 Calories; 17.0 g Total Fat (5.0 g Mono, 1.0 g Poly, 7.0 g Sat); 180 mg Cholesterol;
21 g Carbohydrate; 2 g Fibre; 21 g Protein; 1290 mg Sodium*

Pictured on page 35.

Pizza Calzones

Tasty hand-held turnovers are always a hit with the youngsters. This delicious lunch option packs in all those popular pizza toppings for a sure-fire favourite.

Cooking oil	2 tsp.	10 mL
Chopped fresh white mushrooms	1 cup	250 mL
Chopped green pepper	1/2 cup	125 mL
Chopped onion	1/2 cup	125 mL
Dried crushed chilies	1/4 tsp.	1 mL
Pizza sauce	1/2 cup	125 mL
Chopped black olives	2 tbsp.	30 mL
Grated Italian cheese blend	1 1/2 cups	375 mL
Sliced deli pepperoni sticks (1/4 inch, 6 mm, thick)	3/4 cup	175 mL
Large egg, fork-beaten	1	1
Water	1 tbsp.	15 mL
Frozen white bread dough, covered, thawed in refrigerator overnight	1	1

Heat cooking oil in medium frying pan on medium. Add next 4 ingredients. Cook for about 8 minutes, stirring occasionally, until onion is softened. Remove from heat.

Stir in pizza sauce and olives. Transfer to medium bowl. Let stand for 10 minutes.

Add cheese and pepperoni. Stir well.

Combine egg and water in small bowl. Divide dough into 8 equal portions. Roll out 1 portion on lightly floured surface to 6 inch (15 cm) diameter circle. Spoon about 1/4 cup (60 mL) filling on half of circle, leaving 1/2 inch (12 mm) edge. Brush edge of dough with egg mixture. Fold dough over pepperoni mixture. Crimp edges with fork or pinch together to seal. Repeat with remaining dough and pepperoni mixture. Arrange, about 2 inches (5 cm) apart, on greased baking sheet. Brush with remaining egg mixture. Cut 2 or 3 small slits in tops to allow steam to escape. Bake in 375°F (190°C) oven for about 22 minutes until golden. Makes 8 calzones.

1 calzone: 310 Calories; 14.0 g Total Fat (4.0 g Mono, 1.5 g Poly, 5.0 g Sat); 45 mg Cholesterol; 33 g Carbohydrate; 2 g Fibre; 13 g Protein; 900 mg Sodium

Pictured on page 35.

Minestrone

An Italian classic. Every region is known to have its own variation—and this delightful version pulls influences from a few of them. Use spinach in place of arugula if you prefer. Add a sprinkle of Parmesan for the perfect finishing touch.

Bacon slices, chopped	3	3
Shredded cabbage, lightly packed	2 cups	500 mL
Chopped carrot	1 cup	250 mL
Chopped onion	1 cup	250 mL
Sliced celery	1 cup	250 mL
Garlic clove, minced (or 1/4 tsp., 1 mL, powder)	1	1
Prepared vegetable broth	5 cups	1.25 L
Can of diced tomatoes (with juice)	28 oz.	796 mL
Can of white kidney beans, rinsed and drained	19 oz.	540 mL
Small shell pasta	1/2 cup	125 mL
Tomato paste (see Tip, below)	2 tbsp.	30 mL
Granulated sugar	1 tsp.	5 mL
Dried thyme	1/2 tsp.	2 mL
Bay leaf	1	1
Arugula, lightly packed	1 cup	250 mL

Cook bacon in Dutch oven on medium until almost crisp. Add next 5 ingredients. Cook for about 10 minutes, stirring often, until carrot starts to soften.

Add next 8 ingredients. Stir. Bring to a boil. Reduce heat to medium-low. Simmer, partially covered, for about 10 minutes until pasta is tender but firm. Remove and discard bay leaf.

Add arugula. Stir. Makes about 12 cups (3 L).

1 cup (250 mL): 120 Calories; 4.0 g Total Fat (1.5 g Mono, 0.5 g Poly, 1.5 g Sat); 5 mg Cholesterol; 18 g Carbohydrate; 3 g Fibre; 5 g Protein; 610 mg Sodium

 tip If a recipe calls for less than an entire can of tomato paste, freeze the unopened can for 30 minutes. Open both ends and push the contents through one end. Slice off only what you need. Freeze the remaining paste in a resealable freezer bag or plastic wrap for future use.

Fennel Orange Salad

If fennel still seems a bit foreign to you and your family, this lovely salad may provide the perfect introduction. Light licorice flavours from fennel combine nicely with fresh spinach, orange and a light homemade dressing.

Olive oil	2 tbsp.	30 mL
Balsamic vinegar	1 tbsp.	15 mL
Liquid honey	1 tbsp.	15 mL
Orange juice	1 tbsp.	15 mL
Dijon mustard	2 tsp.	10 mL
Salt	1/8 tsp.	0.5 mL
Pepper	1/8 tsp.	0.5 mL
Thinly sliced fennel bulb (white part only)	4 cups	1 L
Fresh spinach leaves, lightly packed	3 cups	750 mL
Medium oranges, segmented (see Tip, page 141)	3	3
Thinly sliced red onion	1/4 cup	60 mL

Whisk first 7 ingredients in large bowl.

Add remaining 4 ingredients. Toss. Makes about 9 cups (2.25 L).

1 cup (250 mL): 80 Calories; 3.5 g Total Fat (2.0 g Mono, 0 g Poly, 0 g Sat); 0 mg Cholesterol; 14 g Carbohydrate; 3 g Fibre; 1 g Protein; 70 mg Sodium

 Fennel is frequently found in Italian cuisine. This favourite is known for its light licorice flavours with a delicate sweetness. Fennel seed is also commonly used in cooking and adds a similar licorice flavour that's used in both sweet and savoury applications.

Italian Wedding Soup

So much is lost in translation. The name of this soup, originally known as
minestra maritata, refers to the fact that the ingredients go well together.
Though perhaps not married, nor necessarily served at weddings, this soup is
undoubtedly delicious.

Large egg, fork-beaten	1	1
Fine dry bread crumbs	1/4 cup	60 mL
Garlic clove, minced (or 1/4 tsp., 1 mL, powder)	1	1
Pepper	1/4 tsp.	1 mL
Hot Italian sausage, casing removed	1 lb.	454 g
Olive oil	2 tsp.	10 mL
Chopped celery	1 cup	250 mL
Chopped onion	1 cup	250 mL
Chopped parsnip	1 cup	250 mL
Finely chopped kale leaves, lightly packed (see Tip, page 31)	1 cup	250 mL
Prepared chicken broth	6 cups	1.5 L
Chopped broccoli	2 cups	500 mL
Water	2 cups	500 mL

Combine first 4 ingredients in medium bowl.

Add sausage. Mix well. Roll into 3/4 inch (2 cm) balls. Arrange on greased
baking sheet with sides. Cook in 350°F (175°C) oven for about 10 minutes
until no longer pink inside. Transfer to paper towel-lined plate to drain.

Heat olive oil in Dutch oven on medium. Add next 4 ingredients. Cook for
about 12 minutes, stirring often, until onion is softened.

Add remaining 3 ingredients and meatballs. Bring to a boil. Reduce heat to
medium. Boil gently, partially covered, for about 8 minutes until broccoli
and kale are tender. Makes about 11 cups (2.75 L).

1 cup (250 mL): 197 Calories; 14.0 g Total Fat (1.0 g Mono, 0 g Poly, 4.5 g Sat); 45 mg Cholesterol;
10 g Carbohydrate; 2 g Fibre; 9 g Protein; 730 mg Sodium

Acqua Cotta

If you can boil water, you can make this soup. Literally translated, the recipe title means "cooked water." The toasted bread soaks up the liquid and gives this hearty dish an almost stew-like consistency.

Olive oil	1 tbsp.	15 mL
Chopped onion	1 cup	250 mL
Garlic cloves, thinly sliced	2	2
Salt	1/4 tsp.	1 mL
Pepper	1/4 tsp.	1 mL
Can of diced tomatoes (with juice)	28 oz.	796 mL
Prepared chicken (or vegetable) broth	3 cups	750 mL
Balsamic vinegar	1 tbsp.	15 mL
Calabrese (or ciabatta) bread slices (1/2 inch, 12 mm, thick), toasted	4	4
Grated Parmesan cheese	1/4 cup	60 mL
Chopped fresh basil	2 tbsp.	30 mL

Heat olive oil in large saucepan on medium-high. Add next 4 ingredients. Cook for about 3 minutes, stirring often, until onion starts to brown.

Add next 3 ingredients. Stir. Bring to a boil. Reduce heat to medium-low. Simmer, uncovered, for about 12 minutes, stirring occasionally, until onion is tender.

Arrange toast slices in 4 soup bowls. Spoon tomato mixture over top.

Sprinkle with cheese and basil. Serves 4.

1 serving: 200 Calories; 6.0 g Total Fat (3.0 g Mono, 0.5 g Poly, 1.5 g Sat); 5 mg Cholesterol; 30 g Carbohydrate; 2 g Fibre; 7 g Protein; 1290 mg Sodium

 tip To remove the centre rib from kale, fold the leaf in half along the rib and then cut along the length of the rib. To store, place leaves in large freezer bag. Once frozen, crumble in bag.

Panzanella

Salads need not always contain primarily leafy greens. Panzanella (pronounced pahn-zah-NEHL-lah) has long been enjoyed in Italian cuisine. It is made largely of bread, with vegetables adding flavour and interest.

Calabrese (or ciabatta) bread cubes (3/4 inch, 2 cm, pieces)	4 cups	1 L
Olive oil	2 tbsp.	30 mL
Lemon juice	3 tbsp.	50 mL
Olive oil	3 tbsp.	50 mL
Granulated sugar	2 tsp.	10 mL
Grated lemon zest (see Tip, page 94)	1/2 tsp.	2 mL
Salt	1/2 tsp.	2 mL
Pepper	1/2 tsp.	2 mL
Dried oregano	1/4 tsp.	1 mL
Cut or torn romaine lettuce hearts, lightly packed	4 cups	1 L
Chopped English cucumber (with peel), 3/4 inch (2 cm) pieces	1 1/2 cups	375 mL
Chopped tomato (3/4 inch, 2 cm, pieces)	1 1/2 cups	375 mL
Sliced green onion	3 tbsp.	50 mL

Toss bread cubes in first amount of olive oil in large bowl until coated. Arrange in single layer on ungreased baking sheet with sides. Bake in 350°F (175°C) oven for about 12 minutes, stirring at halftime, until bread starts to turn golden. Let stand on baking sheet on wire rack until cool.

Stir next 7 ingredients in same large bowl until sugar is dissolved.

Add remaining 4 ingredients and bread cubes. Toss. Serve immediately. Makes about 10 cups (2.5 L).

1 cup (250 mL): 110 Calories; 7.0 g Total Fat (5.0 g Mono, 1.0 g Poly, 1.0 g Sat); 0 mg Cholesterol; 10 g Carbohydrate; trace Fibre; 2 g Protein; 115 mg Sodium

Pictured on page 36.

Roasted Potato Salad

Potato salad may not seem like traditional Italian fare, but this version integrates many influences from popular Italian cuisine. Serve while the potatoes are still hot, or cool the potatoes before adding to the other ingredients.

Red baby potatoes, halved	1 1/2 lbs.	680 g
Olive oil	1 tbsp.	15 mL
Salt	1/4 tsp.	1 mL
Pepper, sprinkle		
Olive oil	1/4 cup	60 mL
Lemon juice	3 tbsp.	50 mL
Chopped fresh parsley	2 tbsp.	30 mL
Chopped fresh basil (or 3/4 tsp., 4 mL, dried)	1 tbsp.	15 mL
Liquid honey	1 1/2 tsp.	7 mL
Chopped fresh thyme (or 1/4 tsp., 1 mL, dried)	1 tsp.	5 mL
Salt	1/4 tsp.	1 mL
Pepper	1/8 tsp.	0.5 mL
Grape tomatoes	2 cups	500 mL
Thinly sliced radicchio, lightly packed	1 cup	250 mL
Large hard-cooked eggs, chopped	4	4
Capers	2 tbsp.	30 mL
Bacon slices, cooked crisp and crumbled	3	3

Toss first 4 ingredients in large bowl until coated. Arrange in single layer on greased baking sheet with sides. Cook in 400°F (205°C) oven for about 30 minutes, stirring occasionally, until potatoes are tender.

Whisk next 8 ingredients in same large bowl.

Add remaining 5 ingredients and potatoes. Stir. Makes about 7 cups (1.75 L).

1 cup (250 mL): 240 Calories; 14.0 g Total Fat (9.0 g Mono, 1.5 g Poly, 2.5 g Sat); 125 mg Cholesterol; 22 g Carbohydrate; 2 g Fibre; 8 g Protein; 330 mg Sodium

Pictured on page 36.

Italian Garden Salad

A refreshing and lovely start to any meal, this light green salad includes many tasty Italian ingredients with a homemade dressing to pull it all together.

Mayonnaise	2 tbsp.	30 mL
White balsamic (or white wine) vinegar	2 tbsp.	30 mL
Granulated sugar	1 tsp.	5 mL
Olive oil	1 tsp.	5 mL
Italian seasoning	1/4 tsp.	1 mL
Salt, just a pinch		
Pepper, just a pinch		
Romaine lettuce mix, lightly packed	6 cups	1.5 L
Seasoned croutons	1 cup	250 mL
Halved grape tomatoes	1/2 cup	125 mL
Thinly sliced red onion	1/4 cup	60 mL
Small pitted black olives	1/4 cup	60 mL
Grated Parmesan cheese	1/4 cup	60 mL

Combine first 7 ingredients in large bowl.

Add next 5 ingredients. Toss.

Sprinkle with cheese. Makes about 7 cups (1.75 L).

1 cup (250 mL): 100 Calories; 7.0 g Total Fat (2.0 g Mono, 0 g Poly, 1.5 g Sat); trace Cholesterol; 7 g Carbohydrate; 1 g Fibre; 3 g Protein; 200 mg Sodium

1. Muffuletta Strata, page 26
2. Breakfast Tiramisu, page 25
3. Pizza Calzones, page 27

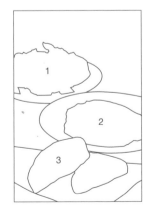

Tuna Chickpea Tomato Salad

It's tough to criticize perfection. This refreshing salad packs fresh veggie flavours with a good punch of protein from chickpeas and tuna. Serve with crusty bread and you could call it a complete meal.

Olive oil	3 tbsp.	50 mL
Lemon juice	2 tbsp.	30 mL
Garlic clove, minced (or 1/4 tsp., 1 mL, powder)	1	1
Salt	1/4 tsp.	1 mL
Pepper	1/4 tsp.	1 mL
Can of chickpeas (garbanzo beans), rinsed and drained	19 oz.	540 mL
Grape tomatoes, halved	1 1/2 cups	375 mL
Chopped arugula, lightly packed	1 cup	250 mL
Can of chunk light tuna in water, drained	6 oz.	170 g
Finely chopped orange pepper	1/2 cup	125 mL
Chopped fresh parsley	3 tbsp.	50 mL
Finely chopped onion	3 tbsp.	50 mL

Whisk first 5 ingredients in large bowl.

Add remaining 7 ingredients. Stir. Makes about 6 cups (1.5 L).

1 cup (250 mL): 146 Calories; 8.0 g Total Fat (5.0 g Mono, 1.0 g Poly, 1.0 g Sat); 10 mg Cholesterol; 11 g Carbohydrate; 3 g Fibre; 8 g Protein; 280 mg Sodium

Pictured at left.

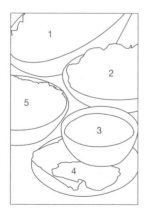

1. Panzanella, page 32
2. Roasted Potato Salad, page 33
3. Pasta e Fagioli, page 38
4. Rosemary Fig Focaccia, page 40
5. Tuna Chickpea Tomato Salad, above

Props: Cherison Enterprises
Out of the Fire Studio

Pasta e Fagioli

This traditional Italian soup is best served with a sprinkle of Parmesan and garlic toast on the side. Pasta e Fagioli (pronounced PAH-stuh eh fah-JYOH-lee) literally translates to "pasta and beans." Any small variety of pasta can be used in place of ditali.

Olive oil	1 tsp.	5 mL
Lean ground beef	1/2 lb.	225 g
Chopped onion	1/2 cup	125 mL
Sliced carrot	1/2 cup	125 mL
Sliced celery	1/2 cup	125 mL
Italian seasoning	1 tbsp.	15 mL
Garlic clove, minced (or 1/4 tsp., 1 mL, powder)	1	1
Can of romano beans, rinsed and drained	19 oz.	540 mL
Prepared beef broth	2 cups	500 mL
Can of diced tomatoes (with juice)	14 oz.	398 mL
Water	1 1/2 cups	375 mL
Can of tomato sauce	7 1/2 oz.	213 mL
Ditali pasta	1/2 cup	125 mL

Heat olive oil in large saucepan on medium. Scramble-fry next 6 ingredients for about 10 minutes until onion is softened.

Mash 1/2 cup (125 mL) beans in small bowl. Add next 4 ingredients, remaining beans and mashed beans to beef mixture. Stir. Bring to a boil. Reduce heat to medium-low. Simmer, partially covered, for 15 minutes, stirring occasionally.

Add pasta. Boil gently, partially covered, for about 15 minutes, stirring occasionally, until pasta is tender but firm. Makes about 8 cups (2 L).

1 cup (250 mL): 178 Calories; 4.5 g Total Fat (2.0 g Mono, 0 g Poly, 1.5 g Sat); 15 mg Cholesterol; 21 g Carbohydrate; 6 g Fibre; 12 g Protein; 610 mg Sodium

Pictured on page 36.

Tomato Bocconcini Salad

Sometimes the simplest recipes yield the most impressive results. This is certainly the case with this recipe, which pulls flavours from the classic caprese (pronounced kah-PRAY-say) salad. Best served with crusty bread.

Medium tomatoes, sliced 1/2 inch (12 mm) thick	4	4
Regular bocconcini (fresh mozzarella), about 2 inch (5 cm) diameter, sliced 1/4 inch (6 mm) thick (see Note)	4	4
Salt	1/4 tsp.	1 mL
Coarsely ground pepper	1/4 tsp.	1 mL
Olive oil	3 tbsp.	50 mL
Finely shredded basil	1 tbsp.	15 mL

Arrange tomato and bocconcini slices, slightly overlapping, in circular pattern on serving plate. Sprinkle with salt and pepper.

Drizzle olive oil over top. Let stand, covered, for 30 minutes.

Sprinkle with basil. Serves 4.

1 serving: 280 Calories; 24.0 g Total Fat (11.0 g Mono, 1.5 g Poly, 10.0 g Sat); 50 mg Cholesterol; 4 g Carbohydrate; trace Fibre; 12 g Protein; 350 mg Sodium

Pictured on page 54.

Note: Use an egg slicer to get perfectly even slices of bocconcini. They can be difficult to slice because they are so soft and round.

 Bocconcini, which literally means "mouthful" in Italian, is also commonly known as fresh mozzarella cheese. These small, round nuggets of cheese are generally very soft and lend their mild flavour to salads, pizzas or any other dish they're added to. Bocconcini is softer than many other varieties of cheese because it's not aged. It's also found packed in water or whey, which further adds to its softness.

Rosemary Fig Focaccia

A simple and straightforward recipe—perfect for those who are new to bread making. This recipe yields an impressive flatbread with lovely flavours of fig and rosemary.

All-purpose flour	3 cups	750 mL
Envelope of instant yeast (or 2 1/4 tsp., 11 mL)	1/4 oz.	8 g
Salt	1 1/2 tsp.	7 mL
Granulated sugar	1 tsp.	5 mL
Very warm water (see Tip, page 41)	1 1/2 cups	375 mL
Finely chopped dried figs	1/3 cup	75 mL
Chopped fresh rosemary (or 3/4 tsp., 4 mL, dried, crushed)	1 tbsp.	15 mL
Olive oil	1 tbsp.	15 mL
Olive oil	1 tbsp.	15 mL
Olive oil	2 tsp.	10 mL
Coarse salt	1/2 tsp.	2 mL

Combine first 4 ingredients in extra-large bowl. Make a well in centre. Add water to well. Stir vigorously until sticky dough forms.

Stir in figs and rosemary. Dough will be wet and sticky. Drizzle with first amount of olive oil. Turn dough to coat all sides. Cover with greased waxed paper and tea towel. Let stand in oven with light on and door closed for about 1 hour until tripled in bulk.

Coat 10 x 15 inch (25 x 38 cm) baking sheet with sides with second amount of olive oil. Gently press dough to fit dimensions of baking sheet. Let stand for 10 minutes.

Poke dough randomly with fork. Brush with third amount of olive oil. Sprinkle with salt. Bake on bottom rack in 450°F (230°C) oven for about 15 minutes until golden. Let stand in pan for 5 minutes before removing to wire rack to cool. Cuts into 12 pieces.

1 piece: 170 Calories; 3.5 g Total Fat (2.5 g Mono, 0 g Poly, 0 g Sat); 0 mg Cholesterol; 32 g Carbohydrate; 2 g Fibre; 4 g Protein; 360 mg Sodium

Pictured on page 36.

Cheese-Stuffed Pizza Crust

Cheese-stuffed pizza crust gets a healthy makeover. Use this crust, stuffed or unstuffed, for Pizza Margherita, page 95.

All-purpose flour	1 1/4 cups	300 mL
Whole-wheat flour	3/4 cup	175 mL
Envelope of instant yeast (or 2 1/4 tsp., 11 mL)	1/4 oz.	8 g
Salt	1 tsp.	5 mL
Very warm water (see Tip, below)	3/4 cup	175 mL
Olive oil	2 tbsp.	30 mL
Mozzarella cheese, cut into 1/4 x 2 1/2 inch (0.6 x 6.4 cm) long sticks	6 oz.	170 g

Combine first 4 ingredients in large bowl. Make a well in centre.

Add water and olive oil to well. Mix until soft dough forms. Turn out onto lightly floured surface. Knead for about 4 minutes until smooth and elastic. Place in greased large bowl, turning once to grease top. Cover with greased waxed paper and tea towel. Let stand at room temperature for 15 minutes. Turn out onto lightly floured surface. Roll out dough to 13 inch (33 cm) circle. Transfer to 12 inch (30 cm) greased pizza pan, allowing excess dough to hang over edge of pan.

Place cheese sticks around dough circle on inside edge of pizza pan. Fold edge of dough over cheese sticks, tucking dough under cheese. Pinch edges to seal. Layer toppings of choice on dough. Bake on bottom rack in 425°F (220°C) oven for about 15 minutes until crust is browned on bottom. Let stand for 5 minutes. Cuts into 8 wedges.

1 wedge (crust only): 210 Calories; 9.0 g Total Fat (4.0 g Mono, 0.5 g Poly, 4.0 g Sat); 20 mg Cholesterol; 24 g Carbohydrate; 2 g Fibre; 8 g Protein; 380 mg Sodium

WHOLE-WHEAT PIZZA CRUST: Omit cheese. Roll out dough to 12 inch (30 cm) circle. Bake as directed.

Pictured on page 90.

 tip When using yeast, it is important for the liquid to be at the correct temperature. If the liquid is too cool, the yeast will not activate properly. If the liquid is too hot, the yeast will be destroyed. For best results, follow the recommended temperatures as instructed on the package.

Mushroom Biscuits

Find mild mushroom flavour in these rustic whole-wheat biscuits. Serve with hearty soups or stews for a satisfying meal.

Package of dried porcini mushrooms (1/2 oz., 14 g)	1/2	1/2
Buttermilk (or soured milk, see Tip, below)	1 1/2 cups	375 mL
Whole-wheat flour	2 cups	500 mL
All-purpose flour	1 cup	250 mL
Baking powder	1 tbsp.	15 mL
Salt	1 tsp.	5 mL
Baking soda	1/2 tsp.	2 mL
Dried thyme	1/2 tsp.	2 mL
Cold butter (or hard margarine), cut up	1/2 cup	125 mL
Grated Asiago cheese	1/4 cup	60 mL
Sliced green onion	1/4 cup	60 mL

Process mushrooms in blender until finely ground. Add buttermilk. Process for 5 seconds. Transfer to medium bowl. Let stand for 10 minutes.

Combine next 6 ingredients in large bowl. Cut in butter until mixture resembles coarse crumbs. Make a well in centre.

Add cheese, green onion and buttermilk mixture to well. Stir until soft dough forms. Turn out onto lightly floured surface. Knead 8 times. Roll or pat out to 3/4 inch (2 cm) thickness. Cut out circles with lightly floured 2 1/2 inch (6.4 cm) biscuit cutter. Arrange about 2 inches (5 cm) apart on greased baking sheet with sides. Bake in 400°F (205°C) oven for about 17 minutes until golden. Let stand on baking sheet for 5 minutes before removing to wire rack to cool. Makes about 17 biscuits.

1 biscuit: 140 Calories; 7.0 g Total Fat (1.5 g Mono, 0 g Poly, 4.0 g Sat); 15 mg Cholesterol; 18 g Carbohydrate; 2 g Fibre; 4 g Protein; 880 mg Sodium

 tip To make soured milk, measure 1 tbsp. (15 mL) white vinegar or lemon juice into a 1 cup (250 mL) liquid measure. Add enough milk to make 1 cup (250 mL). Stir. Let stand for 1 minute.

Gluten-Free Pizza Crust

This gluten-free pizza crust is so simple to make. You can find gluten-free flour and baking powder in major grocery stores or health food stores.

Gluten-free all-purpose baking flour	2 1/4 cups	550 mL
Yellow cornmeal	1/4 cup	60 mL
Gluten-free baking powder	1 tbsp.	15 mL
Xanthan gum (see Note)	2 tsp.	10 mL
Italian seasoning	1 tsp.	5 mL
Baking soda	1/2 tsp.	2 mL
Salt	1/2 tsp.	2 mL
Cold vegetable shortening	1/2 cup	125 mL
Buttermilk (or soured milk, see Tip, page 42)	3/4 cup	175 mL
Gluten-free all-purpose baking flour	1 tbsp.	15 mL

Combine first 7 ingredients in large bowl. Cut in shortening until mixture resembles coarse crumbs. Make a well in centre.

Add buttermilk to well. Stir until just moistened.

Turn out dough onto work surface sprinkled with second amount of flour. Knead 5 times. Press dough into greased 12 inch (30 cm) pizza pan, forming rim around edge. Bake on bottom rack in 400°F (205°C) oven for 10 minutes. Layer toppings of choice on dough. Bake for about 10 minutes until golden. Cuts into 8 wedges.

1 wedge (crust only): 270 Calories; 14.0 g Total Fat (6.0 g Mono, 1.5 g Poly, 5.0 g Sat); 10 mg Cholesterol; 32 g Carbohydrate; 4 g Fibre; 5 g Protein; 420 mg Sodium

Note: Xanthan gum can be found in health food stores, or in the gluten-free or health food aisle in major grocery stores.

Polenta Olive Panbread

A flavourful cornbread that's filled with sun-dried tomatoes, olives and Parmesan cheese. Goes great with soup or salad for a satisfying lunch.

All-purpose flour	1 1/2 cups	375 mL
Yellow cornmeal	1 cup	250 mL
Baking powder	2 tsp.	10 mL
Italian seasoning	1 tsp.	5 mL
Baking soda	1/2 tsp.	2 mL
Salt	1/2 tsp.	2 mL
Garlic powder	1/4 tsp.	1 mL
Large eggs	2	2
Buttermilk (or soured milk, see Tip, page 42)	1 1/3 cups	325 mL
Olive oil	1/3 cup	75 mL
Liquid honey	1 tbsp.	15 mL
Finely chopped black olives	1/2 cup	125 mL
Finely chopped sun-dried tomatoes in oil, blotted dry	1/4 cup	60 mL
Grated Parmesan cheese	1/4 cup	60 mL

Combine first 7 ingredients in large bowl. Make a well in centre.

Beat next 4 ingredients in medium bowl. Add to well.

Add remaining 3 ingredients. Stir until just moistened. Spread evenly in greased 9 x 9 inch (23 x 23 cm) pan. Bake in 350°F (175°C) oven for about 30 minutes until wooden pick inserted in centre comes out clean. Let stand in pan for 10 minutes before removing to wire rack to cool. Cuts into 12 pieces.

1 piece: 210 Calories; 9.0 g Total Fat (6.0 g Mono, 1.0 g Poly, 1.5 g Sat); 25 mg Cholesterol; 27 g Carbohydrate; trace Fibre; 5 g Protein; 340 mg Sodium

Walnut Raisin Rolls

Rustic brown buns filled with raisins and nuts make a perfect choice for breakfast or brunch, or even for a snack with afternoon tea.

Warm water (see Tip, page 41)	3/4 cup	175 mL
Liquid honey	1/2 tsp.	2 mL
Active dry yeast	1 1/2 tsp.	7 mL
Large egg	1	1
Liquid honey	2 tbsp.	30 mL
Olive oil	2 tbsp.	30 mL
Salt	1 tsp.	5 mL
Whole-wheat flour	2 1/2 cups	625 mL
Chopped dark raisins	2/3 cup	150 mL
Chopped walnuts, toasted (see Tip, page 46)	2/3 cup	150 mL
Whole-wheat flour, approximately	1/3 cup	75 mL

Stir water and honey in large bowl until combined. Sprinkle with yeast. Let stand for 10 minutes. Stir until yeast is dissolved.

Add next 4 ingredients. Whisk until smooth.

Add first amount of flour, 1/2 cup (125 mL) at a time, mixing until soft dough forms. Add raisins and walnuts. Mix. Turn out onto lightly floured surface. Knead for 5 to 10 minutes until smooth and elastic, adding second amount of flour 1 tbsp. (15 mL) at a time, if necessary, to prevent sticking. Place in greased extra-large bowl, turning once to grease top. Cover with greased waxed paper and tea towel. Let stand in oven with light on and door closed for about 1 hour until doubled in bulk. Punch dough down. Turn out onto lightly floured surface. Knead for about 1 minute until smooth. Divide dough into 12 equal portions. Roll into balls. Arrange in greased 9 x 13 inch (23 x 33 cm) pan. Cover with greased waxed paper and tea towel. Let stand in oven with light on and door closed for about 1 hour until doubled in size. Bake in 350°F (175°C) oven for about 25 minutes until golden and hollow-sounding when tapped. Remove buns from pan and place on wire rack to cool. Makes 12 buns.

1 bun: 200 Calories; 7.0 g Total Fat (2.5 g Mono, 3.5 g Poly, 1.0 g Sat); 10 mg Cholesterol; 32 g Carbohydrate; 4 g Fibre; 6 g Protein; 210 mg Sodium

Hazelnut Cornmeal Muffins

These lovely cornmeal muffins combine a few unexpected ingredients for a truly spectacular result. Ricotta cheese adds a touch of sweetness, and hazelnuts add both flavour and crunch. Guaranteed to be a favourite.

All-purpose flour	1 1/3 cups	325 mL
Yellow cornmeal	1 cup	250 mL
Granulated sugar	2/3 cup	150 mL
Baking powder	2 tsp.	10 mL
Baking soda	1 tsp.	5 mL
Salt	1/2 tsp.	2 mL
Large egg, fork-beaten	1	1
Ricotta cheese	1 cup	250 mL
Butter (or hard margarine), melted	1/4 cup	60 mL
Milk	1/4 cup	60 mL
Flaked hazelnuts (filberts), toasted (see Tip, below)	1/2 cup	125 mL

Combine first 6 ingredients in large bowl. Make a well in centre.

Beat next 4 ingredients in small bowl. Add to well.

Add hazelnuts. Stir until just moistened. Fill 12 greased muffin cups 3/4 full. Bake in 375°F (190°C) oven for about 17 minutes until wooden pick inserted in centre of muffin comes out clean. Let stand in pan for 5 minutes before removing to wire rack to cool. Makes 12 muffins.

1 muffin: 230 Calories; 8.0 g Total Fat (3.0 g Mono, 0.5 g Poly, 3.5 g Sat); 30 mg Cholesterol; 34 g Carbohydrate; trace Fibre; 6 g Protein; 330 mg Sodium

Pictured on page 53.

 tip When toasting nuts, seeds or coconut, cooking times will vary for each type of nut—so never toast them together. For small amounts, place ingredient in an ungreased frying pan. Heat on medium for 3 to 5 minutes, stirring often, until golden. For larger amounts, spread ingredient evenly in an ungreased shallow pan. Bake in a 350°F (175°C) oven for 5 to 10 minutes, stirring or shaking often, until golden.

Sicilian Fruitbread

This simple, quick bread incorporates pistachios and ricotta cheese, which are often associated with Sicilian cannoli and other southern Italian sweets.

All-purpose flour	2 1/2 cups	625 mL
Granulated sugar	1/2 cup	125 mL
Baking powder	1 1/2 tsp.	7 mL
Baking soda	1 tsp.	5 mL
Ground allspice	1/2 tsp.	2 mL
Ground cinnamon	1/4 tsp.	1 mL
Salt	1/4 tsp.	1 mL
Large egg, fork-beaten	1	1
Orange juice	1 cup	250 mL
Ricotta cheese	1 cup	250 mL
Chopped glazed pineapple	1/2 cup	125 mL
Chopped pistachios	1/2 cup	125 mL
Cooking oil	1/4 cup	60 mL
Cut mixed peel	1/4 cup	60 mL
Icing (confectioner's) sugar	1/2 cup	125 mL
Orange juice	1 tbsp.	15 mL

Combine first 7 ingredients in large bowl. Make a well in centre.

Combine next 7 ingredients in medium bowl. Add to well. Stir until just moistened. Spread evenly in greased 9 x 5 x 3 inch (23 x 12.5 x 7.5 cm) loaf pan. Bake in 350°F (175°C) oven for about 1 hour until wooden pick inserted in centre comes out clean. Let stand in pan for 10 minutes before removing to wire rack to cool completely.

Combine icing sugar and second amount of orange juice in small bowl until smooth. Drizzle over loaf. Cuts into 16 slices.

1 slice: 210 Calories; 7.0 g Total Fat (3.5 g Mono, 1.5 g Poly, 1.5 g Sat); 15 mg Cholesterol; 34 g Carbohydrate; 1 g Fibre; 5 g Protein; 180 mg Sodium

Pictured on page 53.

Parmesan Pesto Grissini

Grissini (pronounced gruh-SEE-nee) is the Italian term for breadsticks. This recipe uses only a few ingredients to create a broadly appealing snack, appetizer or companion for a warm bowl of soup.

Package of puff pastry, thawed according to package directions	14 oz.	397 g
Basil pesto	1/4 cup	60 mL
Balsamic vinegar	1 tbsp.	15 mL
Grated Parmesan cheese	1/2 cup	125 mL
Large egg, fork-beaten	1	1

Roll out half of pastry on lightly floured surface to 8 x 14 inch (20 x 35 cm) rectangle. Chill remaining pastry.

Combine pesto and vinegar in small bowl. Spread over pastry. Sprinkle with cheese. Roll out remaining pastry on lightly floured surface to 8 x 14 inch (20 x 35 cm) rectangle. Place over cheese. Roll gently with rolling pin to press together. Cut crosswise into twenty-four 1/2 x 8 inch (1.2 x 20 cm) strips. Loosely twist strips. Arrange about 2 inches (5 cm) apart, on parchment paper-lined baking sheets.

Brush with egg. Bake in 400°F (205°C) oven for about 20 minutes until puffed and golden. Makes 24 grissini.

1 grissini: 120 Calories; 8.0 g Total Fat (4.0 g Mono, 1.0 g Poly, 2.0 g Sat); 10 mg Cholesterol; 8 g Carbohydrate; 0 g Fibre; 2 g Protein; 95 mg Sodium

Pictured on page 53.

 It is generally felt that no Italian meal is complete without bread—whether that is a softer variety like focaccia or a harder type like grissini. There are many different types of Italian breads, so you should probably make a trip to the *panetteria*, or bakery, before serving up your Italian feast.

Caesar's Crown

All hail this delectable garlic bread in the shape of an ancient Roman laurel wreath.

Frozen whole-wheat (or white) bread dough, covered, thawed in refrigerator overnight	1	1
Crushed seasoned croutons	1 cup	250 mL
Grated Parmesan cheese	1/2 cup	125 mL
Caesar dressing	1/3 cup	75 mL
Large egg, fork-beaten	1	1

Roll out dough on lightly floured surface to 8 x 16 inch (20 x 40 cm) rectangle.

Combine next 3 ingredients in small bowl. Spread over dough, leaving 3/4 inch (2 cm) edge on both long sides. Roll up tightly, jelly-roll style, starting from long edge. Pinch seam against roll to seal. Bend to form horseshoe shape. Place, seam-side down, on greased baking sheet. Using scissors, cut roll 12 times from outside edge to within 1/2 inch (12 mm) of centre. Turn each cut piece on its side, all in the same direction, allowing them to overlap. Cover with greased waxed paper and tea towel. Let stand in oven with light on and door closed for about 1 hour until doubled in size.

Brush with egg. Bake in 350°F (175°C) oven for about 25 minutes until golden and hollow-sounding when tapped. Remove bread from baking sheet and place on wire rack to cool. Cuts into 13 pieces.

1 piece: 160 Calories; 7.0 g Total Fat (2.0 g Mono, 3.0 g Poly, 1.5 g Sat); 15 mg Cholesterol; 20 g Carbohydrate; 2 g Fibre; 5 g Protein; 290 mg Sodium

Pictured on page 53.

Saucy Braised Beef Ribs

Braising may be a little time consuming, but results in tender, flavourful ribs. They're well worth the wait! Serve the delicious sauce over polenta or pasta for a complete meal.

Racks of beef back ribs, bone-in (2 – 3 lbs., 900 g – 1.4 kg, each), trimmed of fat and cut into 1-bone portions	2	2
Pepper	1/2 tsp.	2 mL
Sliced onion	2 cups	500 mL
Sliced carrot	1 cup	250 mL
Bay leaves	2	2
Prepared beef broth	2 cups	500 mL
Dry (or alcohol-free) red wine	1 cup	250 mL
All-purpose flour	2 tbsp.	30 mL
Dijon mustard	2 tbsp.	30 mL
Italian seasoning	1/2 tsp.	2 mL
Balsamic vinegar	1/2 tsp.	2 mL

Arrange ribs, meat-side up, in large roasting pan. Sprinkle with pepper. Cook, uncovered, in 450°F (230°C) oven for about 40 minutes until ribs are browned. Drain and discard fat from pan. Reduce heat to 350°F (175°C).

Scatter next 3 ingredients around ribs.

Whisk next 5 ingredients in medium bowl until smooth. Pour over ribs and vegetables. Stir. Cook, covered, for about 2 hours, turning ribs at halftime, until meat is tender and starts to pull away from bones. Transfer ribs to serving platter. Cover to keep warm. Remove and discard bay leaves from onion mixture. Skim and discard fat from cooking liquid. Transfer to blender or food processor.

Add vinegar. Carefully process until smooth (see Safety Tip). Makes about 2 cups (500 mL) sauce. Serve with ribs. Serves 6.

1 serving: 609 Calories; 31.0 g Total Fat (13.0 g Mono, 1.0 g Poly, 13.0 g Sat); 145 mg Cholesterol; 11 g Carbohydrate; 1 g Fibre; 11 g Protein; 541 mg Sodium

Safety Tip: Follow manufacturer's instructions for processing hot liquids.

Rosemary Beef Stew

Find rosemary flavour front-and-centre in this hearty beef stew. For a more subtle flavour, use only one sprig of fresh rosemary or half the amount of dried.

Olive oil	2 tsp.	10 mL
Boneless beef cross-rib roast, trimmed of fat and cut into 1 inch (2.5 cm) cubes	2 lbs.	900 g
Olive oil	1 tsp.	5 mL
Chopped onion	2 cups	500 mL
Salt	1/4 tsp.	1 mL
Pepper	1/8 tsp.	0.5 mL
Prepared beef broth	3 cups	750 mL
Chopped carrot	2 cups	500 mL
Chopped peeled potato	2 cups	500 mL
Can of tomato paste	5 1/2 oz.	156 mL
Balsamic vinegar	1/4 cup	60 mL
Minute tapioca	1 tbsp.	15 mL
Granulated sugar	1 tsp.	5 mL
Garlic cloves, minced (or 3/4 tsp., 4 mL, powder)	3	3
Sprigs of fresh rosemary (or 3/4 tsp., 4 mL, dried, crushed)	2	2
Bay leaf	1	1
Chopped fresh parsley	2 tbsp.	30 mL

Heat first amount of olive oil in Dutch oven on medium-high. Cook beef in 2 batches, for about 3 minutes per batch, stirring occasionally, until browned. Transfer beef to plate. Reduce heat to medium.

Heat second amount of olive oil in same pot. Add next 3 ingredients. Cook for about 10 minutes, stirring often, until onion is caramelized.

Add next 10 ingredients and beef. Stir. Bring to a boil. Reduce heat to medium-low. Simmer, covered, for about 1 1/2 hours, stirring occasionally, until beef is tender. Remove and discard rosemary sprigs and bay leaf.

Add parsley. Stir. Makes about 8 cups (2 L).

1 cup (250 mL): 300 Calories; 12.0 g Total Fat (6.0 g Mono, 0.5 g Poly, 4.0 g Sat); 75 mg Cholesterol; 21 g Carbohydrate; 3 g Fibre; 36 g Protein; 460 mg Sodium

Pizza Meatloaf

Ever-popular pizza flavours in convenient meatloaf form. Sure to become a favourite with the kids.

Large egg, fork-beaten	1	1
Crushed seasoned croutons	2/3 cup	150 mL
Finely chopped green pepper	1/2 cup	125 mL
Pizza sauce	1/2 cup	125 mL
Finely chopped onion	1/4 cup	60 mL
Thinly sliced deli pepperoni sticks	1/4 cup	60 mL
Chopped fresh basil (or 1 1/2 tsp., 7 mL, dried)	2 tbsp.	30 mL
Lean ground beef	2 lbs.	900 g
Pizza sauce	1/2 cup	125 mL
Part-skim mozzarella cheese slices (about 4 oz., 113 g)	6	6
Sliced black olives	2 tbsp.	30 mL

Combine first 7 ingredients in large bowl.

Add beef. Mix well. Shape into 4 x 10 inch (10 x 25 cm) loaf. Place on greased wire rack set in baking sheet with sides. Cook in 375°F (190°C) oven for 1 hour.

Spread pizza sauce over meatloaf. Arrange cheese slices, slightly overlapping, over top. Sprinkle with olives. Cook for about 15 minutes until internal temperature reaches 160°F (71°C). Cuts into 8 slices.

1 slice: 270 Calories; 13.0 g Total Fat (4.5 g Mono, 0.5 g Poly, 5.0 g Sat); 100 mg Cholesterol; 6 g Carbohydrate; trace Fibre; 30 g Protein; 480 mg Sodium

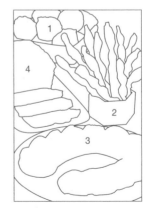

1. Hazelnut Cornmeal Muffins, page 46
2. Parmesan Pesto Grissini, page 48
3. Caesar's Crown, page 49
4. Sicilian Fruitbread, page 47

Props: Cherison Enterprises

Steak Florentine

Though florentine *has come to refer to a dish containing spinach, the term truly means that a dish has been prepared in a style of cooking associated with Florence, Italy. This simple recipe showcases steak's natural flavour.*

Beef rib-eye steaks (about 1 inch, 2.5 cm, thick)	4	4
Coarsely ground pepper	1 tsp.	5 mL
Salt	1/2 tsp.	2 mL
Dried rosemary, crushed	1/4 tsp.	1 mL
Lemon juice	1 tbsp.	15 mL
Olive oil	1 tbsp.	15 mL
Chopped fresh parsley	1 tbsp.	15 mL

Lemon wedges, for garnish

Sprinkle steaks with next 3 ingredients. Preheat gas barbecue to medium-high. Place steaks on greased grill. Close lid. Cook for about 5 minutes per side until internal temperature reaches 160°F (71°C) for medium or until steaks reach desired doneness. Transfer to large plate. Cover with foil. Let stand for 10 minutes.

Drizzle lemon juice and olive oil over steaks. Sprinkle with parsley.

Serve with lemon wedges. Makes 4 steaks.

1/2 steak: 210 Calories; 9.0 g Total Fat (4.0 g Mono, 0 g Poly, 2.5 g Sat); 55 mg Cholesterol; 0 g Carbohydrate; 0 g Fibre; 31 g Protein; 190 mg Sodium

Pictured at left.

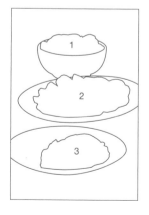

1. Roasted Rosemary Potatoes, page 136
2. Tomato Bocconcini Salad, page 39
3. Steak Florentine, above

Props: Cherison Enterprises
        Danesco

Pizza Wedges

For those who prefer their pizza sans crust, this pizza features toppings only!

Olive oil	2 tsp.	10 mL
Lean ground beef	1 1/2 lbs.	680 g
Olive oil	1 tsp.	5 mL
Grated zucchini (with peel)	1/2 cup	125 mL
Chopped onion	1/4 cup	60 mL
Grated carrot	1/4 cup	60 mL
Italian seasoning	1 tbsp.	15 mL
Garlic clove, minced (or 1/4 tsp., 1 mL, powder)	1	1
Large eggs, fork-beaten	2	2
Fine dry bread crumbs	1/3 cup	75 mL
Grated Parmesan cheese	1/4 cup	60 mL
Can of pizza sauce	7 1/2 oz.	213 mL
Grated mozzarella cheese	1 cup	250 mL
Grated Asiago cheese	1/2 cup	125 mL

Heat first amount of olive oil in large frying pan on medium. Add beef. Scramble-fry for about 10 minutes until no longer pink. Drain. Transfer to large bowl. Set aside.

Heat second amount of olive oil in same frying pan on medium. Add next 5 ingredients. Cook for about 3 minutes, stirring occasionally, until vegetables are softened. Add to beef. Stir. Cool slightly.

Add next 3 ingredients. Mix well. Press into bottom of greased 12 inch (30 cm) deep dish pizza pan. Bake in 400°F (205°C) oven for about 10 minutes until firm.

Spread pizza sauce over beef mixture. Sprinkle with mozzarella and Asiago cheese. Bake for about 15 minutes until cheese is melted and golden. Cuts into 6 wedges.

1 wedge: 370 Calories; 20.0 g Total Fat (6.0 g Mono, 1.5 g Poly, 8.0 g Sat); 145 mg Cholesterol; 10 g Carbohydrate; 1 g Fibre; 36 g Protein; 650 mg Sodium

Beef Ricotta Pie

Creamy, cheesy ricotta tops a saucy mixture of beef, mushrooms and onions. Rich, flavourful and satisfying. Serve with salad and crusty bread to make a complete meal.

Olive oil	2 tsp.	10 mL
Lean ground beef	1 lb.	454 g
Chopped fresh white mushrooms	2 cups	500 mL
Chopped onion	1 cup	250 mL
Garlic cloves, minced (or 1/2 tsp., 2 mL, powder)	2	2
Salt	1/4 tsp.	1 mL
Pepper	1/2 tsp.	2 mL
Can of tomato sauce	14 oz.	398 mL
Balsamic vinegar	1 tbsp.	15 mL
Ricotta cheese	2 cups	500 mL
All-purpose flour	1/4 cup	60 mL
Dried oregano	1/2 tsp.	2 mL
Dried rosemary, crushed	1/2 tsp.	2 mL
Grated Italian cheese blend	1 cup	250 mL

Heat olive oil in large frying pan on medium-high. Add beef. Scramble-fry for about 5 minutes until no longer pink. Drain. Reduce heat to medium.

Add next 5 ingredients. Cook for about 10 minutes, stirring occasionally, until onion is softened.

Add tomato sauce and vinegar. Stir. Transfer to ungreased 2 quart (2 L) casserole.

Whisk next 4 ingredients in medium bowl until combined. Stir in cheese. Spread evenly over beef mixture. Bake, uncovered, in 400°F (205°C) oven for about 30 minutes until topping is golden and set. Serves 6.

1 serving: 350 Calories; 16.0 g Total Fat (4.5 g Mono, 0.5 g Poly, 8.0 g Sat); 85 mg Cholesterol; 18 g Carbohydrate; 2 g Fibre; 33 g Protein; 740 mg Sodium

Italian Pot Roast

Good things come to those who wait. A long cooking time makes this recipe perfect for a relaxed weekend. Plenty of tasty sauce to serve over pasta, potatoes or polenta.

Boneless beef blade (or chuck) roast	3 lbs.	1.4 kg
Salt	1/2 tsp.	2 mL
Pepper	1/4 tsp.	1 mL
Olive oil	2 tsp.	10 mL
Bacon slices, chopped	2	2
Chopped onion	1 1/2 cups	375 mL
Chopped celery	1 cup	250 mL
Dried oregano	1 tsp.	5 mL
Garlic cloves, minced (or 1/2 tsp., 2 mL, powder)	2	2
All-purpose flour	1/4 cup	60 mL
Prepared beef broth	2 cups	500 mL
Can of diced tomatoes, drained	28 oz.	796 mL
Dry (or alcohol-free) red wine	1 cup	250 mL
Bay leaves	2	2

Sprinkle roast with salt and pepper. Heat olive oil in Dutch oven on medium-high. Add roast. Cook for about 10 minutes, turning occasionally, until browned on all sides. Transfer to large plate. Reduce heat to medium.

Add bacon to same pot. Cook for about 3 minutes, stirring often, until almost crisp. Add next 4 ingredients. Cook for about 8 minutes, stirring often, until onion starts to soften.

Add flour. Heat and stir for 1 minute.

Slowly add broth, stirring constantly and scraping any brown bits from bottom of pot, until smooth. Add remaining 3 ingredients. Stir. Add roast. Cook, covered, in 300°F (150°C) oven for about 3 1/2 hours until roast is tender. Remove roast to cutting board. Cover with foil. Let stand for 10 minutes. Slice roast. Remove and discard bay leaves from sauce. Skim and discard fat. Makes about 7 cups (1.75 L) sauce. Serve with roast. Serves 10.

1 serving: 420 Calories; 28.0 g Total Fat (12.0 g Mono, 1.5 g Poly, 11.0 g Sat); 100 mg Cholesterol; 10 g Carbohydrate; 1 g Fibre; 26 g Protein; 650 mg Sodium

Basil Bistecca Sandwiches

Bistecca, or steak as it's more commonly known in North America, combines with basil, mushrooms and seasonings in a perfect topping for open-faced sandwiches. Any variety of bread slices can be used.

Olive oil	1 tsp.	5 mL
Beef strip loin steak, thinly sliced crosswise	1 lb.	454 g
Salt	1/8 tsp.	0.5 mL
Pepper	1/8 tsp.	0.5 mL
Olive oil	1 tsp.	5 mL
Sliced fresh brown (or white) mushrooms	1 cup	250 mL
Thinly sliced onion	1/2 cup	125 mL
Garlic clove, minced (or 1/4 tsp., 1 mL, powder)	1	1
Dried crushed chilies	1/8 tsp.	0.5 mL
Prepared beef broth	1 cup	250 mL
All-purpose flour	1 tbsp.	15 mL
Chopped fresh basil (or 1/2 tsp., 2 mL, dried)	2 tsp.	10 mL
Square panini bread (7 inches, 18 cm), halved diagonally	2	2

Heat first amount of olive oil in large frying pan on medium-high. Add beef. Sprinkle with salt and pepper. Cook for about 5 minutes, stirring occasionally, until browned. Transfer to large plate. Cover to keep warm. Reduce heat to medium.

Heat second amount of olive oil in same frying pan. Add next 4 ingredients. Cook for about 5 minutes, stirring often, until onion starts to brown.

Stir broth into flour in small bowl until smooth. Slowly add to mushroom mixture, stirring constantly until boiling and thickened. Add basil and beef. Heat and stir for 1 minute. Remove from heat.

Arrange bread on greased baking sheet. Broil on top rack in oven for about 30 seconds per side until golden. Arrange on 4 serving plates. Top with beef mixture. Serves 4.

1 serving: 370 Calories; 10.0 g Total Fat (5.0 g Mono, 1.0 g Poly, 3.0 g Sat); 55 mg Cholesterol; 34 g Carbohydrate; 2 g Fibre; 32 g Protein; 650 mg Sodium

Parmesan Meatballs Alla Marinara

Serve the sauce and meatballs over spaghetti for a truly crowd-pleasing dish.

MARINARA SAUCE

Olive oil	1 tbsp.	15 mL
Chopped onion	1 cup	250 mL
Garlic cloves, minced (or 3/4 tsp, 4 mL, powder)	3	3
Dried oregano	1 1/2 tsp.	7 mL
Dried basil	1 tsp.	5 mL
Can of plum tomatoes (with juice), broken up	28 oz.	796 mL
Can of crushed tomatoes	14 oz.	398 mL
Granulated sugar	1 tsp.	5 mL
Salt	1/4 tsp.	1 mL
Pepper	1/4 tsp.	1 mL

MEATBALLS

Large egg, fork-beaten	1	1
Grated Parmesan cheese	1/3 cup	75 mL
Fine dry bread crumbs	1/4 cup	60 mL
Garlic clove, minced (or 1/4 tsp., 1 mL, powder)	1	1
Dried basil	1/2 tsp.	2 mL
Salt	1/4 tsp.	1 mL
Pepper	1/4 tsp.	1 mL
Lean ground beef	1 lb.	454 g

Marinara Sauce: Heat olive oil in large saucepan on medium. Add next 4 ingredients. Cook for about 7 minutes, stirring often, until onion is softened.

Add remaining 5 ingredients. Bring to a boil. Reduce heat to medium-low. Simmer, covered, for 15 minutes, stirring occasionally. Process with hand blender until smooth (see Safety Tip). Makes about 4 cups (1 L) sauce.

(continued on next page)

Meatballs: Combine first 7 ingredients in large bowl.

Add beef. Mix well. Roll into 1 inch (2.5 cm) balls. Arrange in single layer on greased baking sheet with sides. Broil on top rack in oven for about 7 minutes until no longer pink inside. Makes about 32 meatballs. Add to Marinara Sauce. Stir. Makes about 6 1/2 cups (1.6 L).

1 cup (250 mL): 220 Calories; 8.0 g Total Fat (3.5 g Mono, 0.5 g Poly, 3.0 g Sat); 70 mg Cholesterol; 16 g Carbohydrate; 3 g Fibre; 21 g Protein; 750 mg Sodium

Safety Tip: Follow manufacturer's instructions for processing hot liquids.

Calabrese Patties

La cucina Calabrese! *These lively patties are packed with flavours from the Calabria region of Italy. Serve in buns, topped with fresh tomato slices, basil and mayonnaise.*

Large egg, fork-beaten	1	1
Crushed seasoned croutons	1/2 cup	125 mL
Grated mozzarella cheese	1/2 cup	125 mL
Finely chopped sun-dried tomatoes in oil, blotted dry	1/4 cup	60 mL
Italian sausage, casing removed	1/2 lb.	225 g
Lean ground beef	1/2 lb.	225 g

Combine first 4 ingredients in large bowl.

Add sausage and beef. Mix well. Divide into 4 equal portions. Shape into 4 inch (10 cm) patties. Place on greased broiler pan. Broil on centre rack in oven for about 6 minutes per side until internal temperature reaches 160°F (71°C). Makes 4 patties.

1 patty: 370 Calories; 27.0 g Total Fat (12.0 g Mono, 3.0 g Poly, 10.0 g Sat); 125 mg Cholesterol; 6 g Carbohydrate; trace Fibre; 25 g Protein; 630 mg Sodium

Artichoke Chicken

Artichoke is a popular ingredient in Italian cuisine. This simple yet satisfying recipe combines artichoke with chicken and sautéed onions for an easy supper that'll quickly become a favourite.

Boneless, skinless chicken breast halves	1 lb.	454 g
Salt	1/8 tsp.	0.5 mL
Pepper	1/8 tsp.	0.5 mL
Olive oil	2 tsp.	10 mL
Can of artichoke hearts, drained and chopped	14 oz.	398 mL
Finely chopped onion	1/2 cup	125 mL
Garlic cloves, minced (or 1/2 tsp., 2 mL, powder)	2	2
Prepared chicken broth	1/2 cup	125 mL
Prepared chicken broth	2 tbsp.	30 mL
Cornstarch	1 tbsp.	15 mL
Lemon juice	1 tbsp.	15 mL

Cut each chicken breast crosswise into 3 equal pieces. Sprinkle with salt and pepper.

Heat olive oil in large frying pan on medium-high. Add chicken. Cook for about 2 minutes per side until browned. Add next 3 ingredients. Cook for about 5 minutes, stirring often, until onion is softened. Reduce heat to medium-low.

Add first amount of broth. Stir. Cook, covered, for about 5 minutes until chicken is no longer pink inside.

Combine remaining 3 ingredients in small cup. Add to chicken mixture. Heat and stir until boiling and thickened. Serves 4.

1 serving: 180 Calories; 3.5 g Total Fat (2.0 g Mono, 0.5 g Poly, 0.5 g Sat); 65 mg Cholesterol; 8 g Carbohydrate; 2 g Fibre; 28 g Protein; 450 mg Sodium

Rosemary Lemon Meatballs

These tender meatballs are infused with rosemary flavour and found in a light lemony sauce. Goes to show that not all Italian meatballs are served in tomato sauce!

Large egg, fork-beaten	1	1
Fine dry bread crumbs	1/2 cup	125 mL
Chopped fresh rosemary	1 tsp.	5 mL
(or 1/4 tsp., 1 mL, dried, crushed)		
Garlic powder	1/4 tsp.	1 mL
Salt	1/2 tsp.	2 mL
Pepper	1/4 tsp.	1 mL
Lean ground chicken thigh	1 lb.	454 g
Olive oil	1 tbsp.	15 mL
All-purpose flour	1 tbsp.	15 mL
Prepared chicken broth	1 cup	250 mL
Dry (or alcohol-free) white wine	1/4 cup	60 mL
Finely chopped green onion	1/4 cup	60 mL
Lemon juice	1 tbsp.	15 mL
Grated lemon zest (see Tip, page 94)	1/2 tsp.	2 mL
Chopped fresh rosemary	1/4 tsp.	1 mL

Combine first 6 ingredients in large bowl.

Add chicken. Mix well. Roll into 1 inch (2.5 cm) balls. Arrange in single layer on greased baking sheet with sides. Broil on top rack in oven for about 7 minutes until no longer pink inside. Makes about 33 meatballs.

Heat olive oil in large saucepan on medium. Add flour. Heat and stir for 1 minute.

Slowly add broth, stirring constantly until smooth. Add wine. Heat and stir until boiling and thickened. Boil gently for 3 minutes.

Add remaining 4 ingredients and meatballs. Stir. Serves 4.

1 serving: 270 Calories; 12.0 g Total Fat (3.0 g Mono, 1.0 g Poly, 3.0 g Sat); 135 mg Cholesterol; 14 g Carbohydrate; 1 g Fibre; 23 g Protein; 630 mg Sodium

Chicken Porcini Risotto

Risotto is so delicious, but really, who has time for all that fussy stirring? This recipe uses an easy oven method that makes it possible to enjoy a delicious risotto any time. Serve with a squeeze of lemon for a fresh burst of flavour.

Prepared chicken broth	2 1/2 cups	625 mL
Dry (or alcohol-free) white wine	1/2 cup	125 mL
Package of dried porcini mushrooms	1/2 oz.	14 g
Arborio rice	1 cup	250 mL
Finely chopped onion	1/2 cup	125 mL
Garlic cloves, minced (or 1/2 tsp., 2 mL, powder)	2	2
Olive oil	2 tsp.	10 mL
Pepper	1/4 tsp.	1 mL
Chopped cooked chicken (see Tip, page 121)	2 cups	500 mL
Finely chopped red pepper	1/2 cup	125 mL
Grated Parmesan cheese	1/2 cup	125 mL
Chopped fresh parsley (or 3/4 tsp., 4 mL, flakes)	1 tbsp.	15 mL

Bring broth and wine to a boil in medium saucepan. Add mushrooms. Stir. Remove from heat. Let stand, covered, for 10 minutes. Remove mushrooms to cutting board with slotted spoon. Chop. Strain liquid through fine sieve into small bowl. Discard solids.

Combine next 5 ingredients in greased shallow 2 quart (2 L) casserole. Add broth mixture. Stir. Bake, covered, in 400°F (205°C) oven for about 30 minutes until rice is tender and liquid is almost absorbed.

Add chicken, red pepper and mushrooms. Stir. Bake, covered, for about 5 minutes until peppers are tender-crisp and mixture is heated through.

Add cheese and parsley. Stir. Makes about 8 cups (2 L).

1 cup (250 mL): 210 Calories; 5.0 g Total Fat (2.0 g Mono, 1.0 g Poly, 1.5 g Sat); 35 mg Cholesterol; 22 g Carbohydrate; 1 g Fibre; 14 g Protein; 280 mg Sodium

Pesto-Stuffed Chicken

Pesto is certainly a popular Italian culinary invention. This recipe hides a delicious filling of pesto and cheese inside tender chicken.

Grated Italian cheese blend	1/4 cup	60 mL
Basil pesto	3 tbsp.	50 mL
Chopped black olives	2 tbsp.	30 mL
Fine dry bread crumbs	2 tbsp.	30 mL
Boneless, skinless chicken breast halves (4 – 6 oz., 113 – 170 g, each)	4	4
Olive oil	1 tsp.	5 mL
Salt	1/4 tsp.	1 mL
Pepper	1/4 tsp.	1 mL

Combine first 4 ingredients in small bowl.

Cut horizontal slits in thickest part of chicken to create pockets. Fill with cheese mixture. Secure with wooden picks.

Combine remaining 3 ingredients in small cup. Rub over chicken. Preheat gas barbecue to medium. Place chicken on greased grill. Close lid. Cook for about 10 minutes per side until internal temperature reaches 170°F (77°C). Remove and discard wooden picks. Makes 4 stuffed chicken breasts.

1 stuffed chicken breast: 280 Calories; 11.0 g Total Fat (2.0 g Mono, 1.0 g Poly, 2.5 g Sat); 100 mg Cholesterol; 4 g Carbohydrate; trace Fibre; 39 g Protein; 490 mg Sodium

fyi Pesto is said to have originated from Genoa, Italy. The term *pesto* literally translates to "pounded," which makes sense since this delectable condiment is traditionally made by crushing herbs, cheese, garlic and pine nuts together using a mortar and pestle. Though many pestos are made in a food processor these days, they still make for a flavourful addition to all sorts of recipes.

Turkey Marsala

This casually elegant main course combines tender turkey with mushrooms and marsala wine. Fairly easy to put together, and goes great with a side of buttered noodles with herbs.

Butter	1 tbsp.	15 mL
Turkey scaloppine	1 lb.	454 g
Salt, sprinkle		
Pepper, sprinkle		
Sliced fresh white mushrooms	2 cups	500 mL
Prepared chicken broth	1 cup	250 mL
Marsala wine	1/4 cup	60 mL
Water	1 tbsp.	15 mL
Cornstarch	2 tsp.	10 mL
Chopped fresh chives	1 tbsp.	15 mL

Melt butter in large frying pan on medium-high. Sprinkle turkey with salt and pepper. Cook turkey in 2 batches for about 2 minutes per batch, turning at halftime, until browned. Transfer to large plate.

Add mushrooms to same frying pan. Cook for about 5 minutes, stirring occasionally, until mushrooms are softened and liquid is evaporated. Add broth and wine. Stir. Bring to a boil.

Stir water into cornstarch in small cup until smooth. Add to mushroom mixture. Heat and stir until boiling and thickened. Add turkey. Reduce heat to medium-low. Simmer, covered, for about 5 minutes, turning turkey occasionally, until heated through.

Sprinkle with chives. Serves 4.

1 serving: 190 Calories; 5.0 g Total Fat (1.5 g Mono, 0.5 g Poly, 2.5 g Sat); 65 mg Cholesterol; 4 g Carbohydrate; 0 g Fibre; 27 g Protein; 240 mg Sodium

Chicken Cacciatore

A hearty homemade cacciatore *recipe with a bright tomato taste. Wine and capers add loads of flavour to this saucy dish that's perfect for serving over pasta or rice.*

Olive oil	1 tbsp.	15 mL
Boneless, skinless chicken thighs, quartered	1 1/2 lbs.	680 g
Sliced fresh white mushrooms	2 cups	500 mL
Chopped onion	1 cup	250 mL
Garlic cloves, minced (or 1/2 tsp., 2 mL, powder)	2	2
Dry (or alcohol-free) red wine	1/2 cup	125 mL
Can of diced tomatoes (with juice)	28 oz.	796 mL
Chopped red pepper	1 1/2 cups	375 mL
Chopped sun-dried tomatoes in oil	1/4 cup	60 mL
Tomato paste (see Tip, page 28)	3 tbsp.	50 mL
Capers	2 tbsp.	30 mL
Dried basil	1 tsp.	5 mL
Dried oregano	1 tsp.	5 mL
Granulated sugar	1/2 tsp.	2 mL
Bay leaf	1	1
Salt	1/2 tsp.	2 mL
Pepper	1/4 tsp.	1 mL

Heat olive oil in large saucepan on medium-high. Add chicken. Cook for about 10 minutes, turning occasionally, until starting to brown. Reduce heat to medium.

Add next 3 ingredients. Cook for about 8 minutes, stirring often, until onion is softened.

Add wine. Cook for 2 minutes, scraping any brown bits from bottom of pot.

Add remaining 11 ingredients. Bring to a boil. Reduce heat to medium-low. Simmer, partially covered, for 25 minutes to blend flavours. Remove and discard bay leaf. Makes about 7 cups (1.75 L).

1 cup (250 mL): 210 Calories; 7.0 g Total Fat (3.0 g Mono, 1.5 g Poly, 1.5 g Sat); 80 mg Cholesterol; 13 g Carbohydrate; 3 g Fibre; 22 g Protein; 720 mg Sodium

Pictured on page 71.

Parmesan Arugula Piccata

Though piccata (pronounced pih-KAH-tuh) is generally a veal dish, it can also be made with chicken. This recipe is classy enough for company, but also a great option for any night of the week.

Large eggs	2	2
Fine dry bread crumbs	3/4 cup	175 mL
Grated Parmesan cheese	2 tbsp.	30 mL
Garlic powder	1/2 tsp.	2 mL
Salt	1/2 tsp.	2 mL
Pepper	3/4 tsp.	4 mL
Chicken breast cutlets	1 1/2 lbs.	680 g
Olive oil	2 tbsp.	30 mL
Finely chopped onion	1/4 cup	60 mL
Finely chopped arugula, lightly packed	1/3 cup	75 mL
Prepared chicken broth	1/3 cup	75 mL

Beat eggs with fork in large shallow bowl.

Combine next 5 ingredients on large plate.

Dip chicken into egg mixture. Press both sides of chicken into crumb mixture until coated. Discard any remaining egg and bread crumb mixtures.

Heat olive oil in large frying pan on medium. Add chicken. Cook for about 5 minutes per side until golden and no longer pink inside. Transfer to large plate. Cover to keep warm.

Add onion to same frying pan. Cook for about 2 minutes, stirring often, until softened and starting to brown.

Add arugula and broth. Heat and stir, scraping any brown bits from bottom of pan, until boiling. Drizzle over chicken. Serves 6.

1 serving: 230 Calories; 8.0 g Total Fat (4.0 g Mono, 1.0 g Poly, 1.5 g Sat); 100 mg Cholesterol; 10 g Carbohydrate; trace Fibre; 29 g Protein; 410 mg Sodium

Pictured on page 71.

Turkey Rissoles

Rissole (pronounced rih-SOHL) can refer to very different dishes depending upon where you are. This Italian-style rissole features turkey patties in a lovely tomato and onion sauce. Serve with rice or crusty bread.

Large egg, fork-beaten	1	1
Fine dry bread crumbs	1/4 cup	60 mL
Salt	1/2 tsp.	2 mL
Pepper	1/4 tsp.	1 mL
Ground cinnamon	1/8 tsp.	0.5 mL
Lean ground turkey thigh	1 lb.	454 g
Olive oil	1 tbsp.	15 mL
Chopped onion	1 cup	250 mL
Finely chopped celery	1/2 cup	125 mL
Garlic cloves, minced (or 1/2 tsp., 2 mL, powder)	2	2
Can of diced tomato (with juice)	14 oz.	398 mL
Prepared chicken broth	1/2 cup	125 mL
Granulated sugar	1/2 tsp.	2 mL

Combine first 5 ingredients in large bowl.

Add turkey. Mix well. Divide into 8 equal portions. Shape into 1/2 inch (12 mm) thick oval-shaped patties.

Heat olive oil in large frying pan on medium. Add patties. Cook for about 3 minutes per side until browned. Transfer to large plate. Cover to keep warm.

Add next 3 ingredients to same frying pan. Cook for about 5 minutes, stirring often, until onion is softened.

Add remaining 3 ingredients. Stir. Bring to a boil. Add patties. Cook, covered, for about 5 minutes until patties are no longer pink inside. Serves 4.

1 serving: 240 Calories; 12.0 g Total Fat (2.5 g Mono, 1.0 g Poly, 1.0 g Sat); 95 mg Cholesterol; 15 g Carbohydrate; 2 g Fibre; 25 g Protein; 840 mg Sodium

Pictured on page 71.

Turkey Prosciutto Rolls

Just a few ingredients combine for a truly amazing result. The rolling takes a little bit of work, but leads to an impressive dish that definitely qualifies as company-worthy fare.

Chopped fresh sage (or 1 1/2 tsp., 7 mL, dried)	2 tbsp.	30 mL
Prosciutto (or deli) ham slices (about 4 oz., 113 g)	8	8
Turkey scaloppine (about 2 oz., 57 g, each)	8	8
Pepper	1/2 tsp.	2 mL
Olive oil	1 tbsp.	15 mL
Prepared chicken broth	1/2 cup	125 mL

Arrange sage and prosciutto over turkey slices. Roll up tightly, jelly-roll style, starting from long edge. Secure with wooden picks. Sprinkle with pepper.

Heat olive oil in large frying pan on medium. Add rolls. Cook for about 8 minutes, turning occasionally, until browned on all sides.

Add broth. Cook, covered, for about 3 minutes until turkey is no longer pink. Remove and discard wooden picks. Makes 8 rolls. Serves 4.

1 turkey roll: 196 Calories; 7.0 g Total Fat (3.5 g Mono, 1.0 g Poly, 2.0 g Sat); 70 mg Cholesterol; trace Carbohydrate; 0 g Fibre; 30 g Protein; 410 mg Sodium

1. Chicken Cacciatore, page 67
2. Parmesan Arugula Piccata, page 68
3. Lemon Garlic Zucchini, page 134
4. Turkey Rissoles, page 69

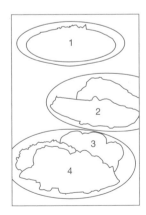

Pepper Prosciutto Shrimp

A spicy blend of prosciutto ham, shrimp, bell peppers and chili paste. This clever recipe uses an easy stir-fry method that'll have dinner on the table in no time. Serve with rice or pasta.

Olive oil	1 tbsp.	15 mL
Chopped onion	1 cup	250 mL
Chopped prosciutto (or deli) ham (about 2 1/2 oz., 70 g)	1/2 cup	125 mL
Chili paste (sambal oelek)	1 tsp.	5 mL
Dried basil	1 tsp.	5 mL
Uncooked medium shrimp (peeled and deveined)	1 lb.	454 g
Chopped red pepper	1/2 cup	125 mL
Chopped orange pepper	1/2 cup	125 mL
Chopped yellow pepper	1/2 cup	125 mL
Lemon juice	1 tbsp.	15 mL
Grated lemon zest (see Tip, page 94)	1/2 tsp.	2 mL
Salt	1/4 tsp.	1 mL
Pepper	1/4 tsp.	1 mL

Heat olive oil in large frying pan on medium-high. Add next 4 ingredients. Cook for about 3 minutes, stirring often, until onion starts to soften.

Add remaining 8 ingredients. Cook for about 5 minutes, stirring often, until shrimp turn pink. Makes about 3 1/2 cups (875 mL).

3/4 cup (175 mL): 180 Calories; 6.0 g Total Fat (2.0 g Mono, 1.5 g Poly, 1.0 g Sat); 150 mg Cholesterol; 8 g Carbohydrate; 1 g Fibre; 23 g Protein; 500 mg Sodium

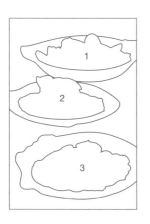

1. Mussels Puttanesca, page 74
2. Pepper-Topped Sole, page 75
3. Scallops Arrabiata, page 76

Mussels Puttanesca

Puttanesca (pronounced poot-tah-NEHS-kah) is an Italian sauce of tomatoes, olives, capers and garlic cooked in olive oil. This recipe uses the flavourful sauce as a base for cooking tasty mussels.

Fresh mussels, scrubbed clean (see Note 1)	3 lbs.	1.4 kg
Olive oil	2 tbsp.	30 mL
Chopped onion	1 cup	250 mL
Garlic cloves, minced (or 1/2 tsp., 2 mL, powder)	2	2
Dried crushed chilies	1/2 tsp.	2 mL
Can of diced tomatoes (with juice)	28 oz.	796 mL
Sliced kalamata olives	1/2 cup	125 mL
Capers	2 tbsp.	30 mL
Red wine vinegar	1 tbsp.	15 mL
Liquid honey	1 tsp.	5 mL
Worcestershire sauce	1 tsp.	5 mL
Dried oregano	1/2 tsp.	2 mL

Put mussels into large bowl. Lightly tap any mussels that are opened 1/4 inch (6 mm) or more. Discard any that do not close (see Note 2).

Heat olive oil in Dutch oven on medium. Add next 3 ingredients. Cook for about 5 minutes, stirring often, until onion is softened.

Add remaining 7 ingredients. Stir. Bring to a boil. Add mussels. Cook, covered, for about 10 minutes, stirring at halftime, until mussels are opened. Discard any unopened mussels. Transfer to serving bowl. Serves 6.

1 serving: 300 Calories; 12.0 g Total Fat (6.0 g Mono, 2.0 g Poly, 1.5 g Sat); 65 mg Cholesterol; 19 g Carbohydrate; 1 g Fibre; 28 g Protein; 1390 mg Sodium

Pictured on page 72.

Note 1: Remove the "beard," the stringy fibres attached to the shell, either by clipping them or giving them a sharp tug out the hinge end of the mussel (not the open end).

Note 2: It is important to discard any mussels that do not close before cooking, as well as any that have not opened during cooking.

Pepper-Topped Sole

A simple main course that uses sweet bell peppers to accentuate mild sole.
Colourful and appetizing, this quick and easy dish is sure to satisfy.

Sole fillets, any small bones removed	1 lb.	454 g
Salt	1/4 tsp.	1 mL
Pepper	1/8 tsp.	0.5 mL
All-purpose flour	1/4 cup	60 mL
Olive oil	1 tbsp.	15 mL
Thinly sliced red pepper	1/2 cup	125 mL
Thinly sliced yellow pepper	1/2 cup	125 mL
Fennel seed	1/2 tsp.	2 mL
Dry (or alcohol-free) white wine	1/2 cup	125 mL
Butter (or hard margarine)	2 tbsp.	30 mL
Chopped fresh parsley	1 tbsp.	15 mL

Sprinkle fillets with salt and pepper. Press into flour on large plate until coated. Discard any remaining flour.

Heat olive oil in large frying pan on medium. Cook fillets in 2 batches for about 2 minutes per batch, turning at halftime, until lightly browned and fish flakes easily when tested with fork. Transfer to serving plate. Cover to keep warm.

Add next 3 ingredients to same frying pan. Cook for about 3 minutes, stirring occasionally, until peppers start to soften. Add wine. Stir. Bring to a boil, scraping any brown bits from bottom of pan. Simmer for 2 minutes. Add butter. Stir until melted. Spoon over fillets.

Sprinkle with parsley. Serves 4.

1 serving: 240 Calories; 11.0 g Total Fat (4.5 g Mono, 1.0 g Poly, 4.5 g Sat); 70 mg Cholesterol; 7 g Carbohydrate; trace Fibre; 22 g Protein; 250 mg Sodium

Pictured on page 72.

Scallops Arrabiata

Arrabiata (pronounced ah-rah-bee-AH-tah) literally translates to "angry."
Culinarily speaking, this term is used to refer to spicy dishes, often containing
pancetta (bacon) and chilies. Serve with crusty bread.

Bacon slices, chopped	4	4
Large sea scallops	1 lb.	454 g
Can of diced tomatoes (with juice)	14 oz.	398 mL
White wine vinegar	1 tbsp.	15 mL
Garlic clove, minced (or 1/4 tsp., 1 mL, powder)	1	1
Dried crushed chilies	1/2 tsp.	2 mL
Granulated sugar	1/4 tsp.	1 mL
Salt	1/8 tsp.	0.5 mL
Pepper	1/8 tsp.	0.5 mL
Finely shredded basil	1 tbsp.	15 mL

Cook bacon in large frying pan on medium until crisp. Transfer with slotted spoon to paper towel-lined plate to drain. Drain and discard all but 2 tsp. (10 mL) drippings.

Add scallops to same frying pan. Cook for about 1 minute per side until browned. Remove to large plate.

Add next 7 ingredients to same frying pan. Cook for 5 minutes, stirring occasionally. Add scallops and bacon. Heat and stir for about 2 minutes until scallops are opaque.

Sprinkle with basil. Makes about 2 1/2 cups (625 mL).

1/2 cup (125 mL): 150 Calories; 5.0 g Total Fat (2.0 g Mono, 0.5 g Poly, 1.5 g Sat);
40 mg Cholesterol; 6 g Carbohydrate; 0 g Fibre; 18 g Protein; 510 mg Sodium

Pictured on page 72.

Cioppino Express

Wine and seafood give this brothy stew decidedly uptown flavours.
Serve accompanied with crusty bread—and more wine (of course).

Olive oil	2 tsp.	10 mL
Chopped onion	1/2 cup	125 mL
Chopped red pepper	1/2 cup	125 mL
Garlic cloves, minced (or 1/2 tsp., 2 mL, powder)	2	2
Dried oregano	1 tsp.	5 mL
Can of diced tomatoes (with juice)	14 oz.	398 mL
Prepared vegetable broth	1 cup	250 mL
Dry (or alcohol-free) white wine	1/2 cup	125 mL
Granulated sugar	1/2 tsp.	2 mL
Worcestershire sauce	1/2 tsp.	2 mL
Salt	1/4 tsp.	1 mL
Bay leaf	1	1
Haddock fillets, any small bones removed, cut into 1 inch (2.5 cm) pieces	1/2 lb.	225 g
Small bay scallops	1/2 lb.	225 g
Uncooked medium shrimp (peeled and deveined)	1/2 lb.	225 g
Chopped fresh parsley (or 3/4 tsp., 4 mL, flakes)	1 tbsp.	15 mL

Heat olive oil in large saucepan on medium. Add onion and red pepper. Cook for about 5 minutes, stirring often, until onion is softened.

Add garlic and oregano. Heat and stir for about 1 minute until garlic is fragrant.

Add next 7 ingredients. Bring to a boil. Boil gently, uncovered, for 10 minutes. Remove and discard bay leaf.

Add next 3 ingredients. Stir. Cook, covered, for about 5 minutes, stirring at halftime, until shrimp turn pink and fish flakes easily when tested with fork.

Sprinkle with parsley. Makes about 5 1/2 cups (1.4 L).

1 cup (250 mL): 180 Calories; 3.0 g Total Fat (1.5 g Mono, 0.5 g Poly, 0 g Sat); 100 mg Cholesterol; 9 g Carbohydrate; trace Fibre; 24 g Protein; 650 mg Sodium

Trout and Fennel Gratinato

A gratin-like topping of fennel, cheese and garlic covers tender trout fillets. Rich and buttery, this is one dish that doesn't cut any corners when it comes to decadence.

Butter (or hard margarine)	3 tbsp.	50 mL
Thinly sliced fennel bulb (white part only)	2 cups	500 mL
Garlic clove, minced (or 1/4 tsp., 1 mL, powder)	1	1
Ground nutmeg	1/8 tsp.	0.5 mL
Rainbow trout fillets, any small bones removed	1 lb.	454 g
Salt	1/8 tsp.	0.5 mL
Pepper	1/8 tsp.	0.5 mL
Grated Romano cheese	1/4 cup	60 mL

Melt butter in small frying pan on medium. Add next 3 ingredients. Cook for about 8 minutes, stirring occasionally, until fennel starts to soften. Remove from heat.

Arrange fillets in single layer in greased 9 x 13 inch (23 x 33 cm) baking dish. Sprinkle with salt and pepper. Spoon fennel mixture over top.

Sprinkle with cheese. Cook in 400°F (205°C) oven for about 10 minutes until fish flakes easily when tested with fork. Serves 4.

1 serving: 240 Calories; 14.0 g Total Fat (4.0 g Mono, 2.0 g Poly, 7.0 g Sat); 95 mg Cholesterol; 4 g Carbohydrate; 1 g Fibre; 25 g Protein; 220 mg Sodium

Basil Basa Bundles

Flavourful basil infuses tender basa. Cooking en papillote (in a parchment paper packet) results in moist, perfectly cooked fish with only minimal effort.

Basa fillets, any small bones removed	1 lb.	454 g
Butter (or hard margarine), melted	1 tbsp.	15 mL
Chopped fresh basil (or 1/2 tsp., 2 mL, dried)	1 tbsp.	15 mL
Lemon juice	1 tbsp.	15 mL
Salt	1/8 tsp.	0.5 mL

(continued on next page)

Cut 4 sheets of parchment paper, each about 12 inches (30 cm) long. Arrange 1 fillet in centre of each sheet.

Combine remaining 4 ingredients in small cup. Drizzle over fillets. Bring edges of parchment together over fillets to enclose. Fold ends together several times to seal completely. Place on baking sheet with sides. Cook in 400°F (205°C) oven for about 10 minutes until fish flakes easily when tested with fork. Makes 4 bundles.

1 bundle: 140 Calories; 6.0 g Total Fat (2.0 g Mono, 1.0 g Poly, 2.5 g Sat); 75 mg Cholesterol; 0 g Carbohydrate; 0 g Fibre; 21 g Protein; 170 mg Sodium

Tuscan Grilled Halibut

Travel to Tuscany without leaving your kitchen. Serve with pasta or salad for a lovely summer meal.

HERB TOMATO MAYO

Mayonnaise	2/3 cup	150 mL
Sun-dried tomato pesto	2 tbsp.	30 mL
Italian seasoning	1 1/2 tsp.	7 mL
Balsamic vinegar	1 tsp.	5 mL
Granulated sugar	1/2 tsp.	2 mL
Salt, just a pinch		

GRILLED HALIBUT

Olive oil	2 tbsp.	30 mL
Balsamic vinegar	1 tbsp.	15 mL
Dijon mustard	1 tsp.	5 mL
Pepper	1/2 tsp.	2 mL
Halibut fillets, any small bones removed	1 lb.	454 g

Herb Tomato Mayo: Stir all 6 ingredients in small bowl until smooth. Chill until ready to serve. Makes about 3/4 cup (175 mL) mayo.

Grilled Halibut: Stir first 4 ingredients in small cup until smooth.

Place fillets in large resealable freezer bag. Add olive oil mixture. Seal bag. Turn until coated. Marinate in refrigerator for 1 hour. Remove fillets. Discard remaining olive oil mixture. Preheat gas barbecue to medium. Place fillets on well-greased grill. Close lid. Cook for about 4 minutes per side until fish flakes easily when tested with fork. Transfer to serving platter. Serve with Herb Tomato Mayo. Serves 4.

1 serving: 430 Calories; 35.0 g Total Fat (1.5 g Mono, 1.0 g Poly, 4.5 g Sat); 50 mg Cholesterol; 2 g Carbohydrate; 0 g Fibre; 24 g Protein; 310 mg Sodium

Salmon Dill Risotto

*Risotto is a widely popular Italian dish. This version combines salmon,
vegetables, wine and seasonings for a nicely flavoured risotto with a cheesy
Romano finish.*

Prepared vegetable broth	5 cups	1.25 L
Olive oil	1 tsp.	5 mL
Chopped onion	1 cup	250 mL
Dried dillweed	1 tsp.	5 mL
Garlic cloves, minced (or 1/2 tsp., 2 mL, powder)	2	2
Salt	1/4 tsp.	1 mL
Pepper	1/4 tsp.	1 mL
Arborio rice	1 1/2 cups	375 mL
Dry (or alcohol-free) white wine	1/2 cup	125 mL
Salmon fillets, skin and any small bones removed, cut into bite-sized pieces	3/4 lb.	340 g
Diced zucchini (with peel)	2 cups	500 mL
Frozen peas, thawed	1 cup	250 mL
Grated Romano cheese	1/2 cup	125 mL

Bring broth to a boil in small saucepan. Reduce heat to low. Cover to keep hot.

Heat olive oil in large saucepan on medium. Add next 5 ingredients. Cook for about 5 minutes, stirring often, until onion is softened.

Add rice. Heat and stir for about 1 minute until rice is coated. Add wine. Heat and stir for about 1 minute until liquid is evaporated. Add 1 cup (250 mL) hot broth, stirring constantly until broth is almost absorbed. Repeat with remaining broth, adding 1 cup (250 mL) at a time. Add next 3 ingredients with last addition of broth. Cook for about 8 minutes, stirring often, until fish flakes easily when tested with fork and rice is tender and creamy.

Add cheese. Stir. Makes about 7 1/2 cups (1.9 L).

1 cup (250 mL): 270 Calories; 4.5 g Total Fat (2.0 g Mono, 1.5 g Poly, 1.5 g Sat); 30 mg Cholesterol; 38 g Carbohydrate; 2 g Fibre; 15 g Protein; 546 mg Sodium

Crispy Parmesan Haddock

This recipe uses just a few ingredients to create a delicious alternative to deep-fried fish. Serve with a wedge of lemon to squeeze over top, which adds a nice dose of freshness.

Large eggs	2	2
Grated Parmesan cheese	3/4 cup	175 mL
Panko (or fine dry) bread crumbs	1 1/2 cups	375 mL
Italian seasoning	1 tsp.	5 mL
Salt	1/4 tsp.	1 mL
Pepper	1/4 tsp.	1 mL
Haddock fillets, any small bones removed, cut lengthwise into 1 inch (2.5 cm) strips	1 lb.	454 g

Cooking spray

Beat eggs in medium bowl. Add cheese. Stir.

Combine next 4 ingredients in large shallow dish.

Dip fish into egg mixture. Press both sides into bread crumb mixture until coated. Arrange on greased baking sheet with sides. Discard any remaining egg and crumb mixtures.

Spray fish with cooking spray. Cook in 450°F (230°C) oven for about 7 minutes until fish flakes easily when tested with fork. Makes about 15 pieces.

1 piece: 70 Calories; 2.0 g Total Fat (0.5 g Mono, 0 g Poly, 1.0 g Sat); 40 mg Cholesterol; 3 g Carbohydrate; 0 g Fibre; 9 g Protein; 140 mg Sodium

 fyi What makes Parmesan cheese so flavourful? This Italian staple is made from cow's milk, then pressed, salted and dried. Parmesan cheese is typically aged for up to two years to fully develop its sharp, complex flavour, while some varieties are aged for up to four years.

Nutty Blue Cheese Chops

Why bother with the fuss of stuffing pork chops when you can just pile the tasty seasonings on top? This recipe features tender pork with a crispy topping of bread crumbs, pine nuts and cheese for a delightfully casual dinner option.

Crumbled blue cheese	1/3 cup	75 mL
Fine dry bread crumbs	1/4 cup	60 mL
Pine nuts, toasted (see Tip, page 46), chopped	3 tbsp.	50 mL
Chopped fresh parsley (or 3/4 tsp., 4 mL, flakes)	1 tbsp.	15 mL
Seasoned salt	1/4 tsp.	1 mL
Pepper	1/4 tsp.	1 mL
Garlic powder	1/8 tsp.	0.5 mL
Boneless centre-cut pork chops (about 1 lb., 454 g)	4	4
Olive oil	1 tbsp.	15 mL

Combine first 4 ingredients in small bowl. Set aside.

Sprinkle next 3 ingredients over both sides of pork chops.

Heat olive oil in large frying pan on medium-high. Add pork chops. Cook for about 2 minutes per side until browned. Transfer to greased baking sheet with sides. Spoon cheese mixture over top. Cook in 400°F (205°C) oven for about 7 minutes until internal temperature of pork reaches 160°F (71°C). Serves 4.

1 serving: 310 Calories; 19.0 g Total Fat (8.0 g Mono, 3.5 g Poly, 5.0 g Sat); 70 mg Cholesterol; 6 g Carbohydrate; trace Fibre; 29 g Protein; 350 mg Sodium

Chili Herb Porchetta

This recipe for porchetta, which is the Italian term for roast pork, is a little fussy since the rolling requires a bit of work. But there's no doubt that the lovely spiral appearance makes this elegant dish worthy of the finest of company.

Boneless pork loin roast	3 lbs.	1.4 kg
Olive oil	3 tbsp.	50 mL
Chopped fresh dill (or 3/4 tsp., 4 mL, dried)	1 tbsp.	15 mL
Chopped fresh rosemary (or 3/4 tsp., 4 mL, dried, crushed)	1 tbsp.	15 mL
Chopped fresh sage (or 3/4 tsp., 4 mL, dried)	1 tbsp.	15 mL
White wine vinegar	1 tbsp.	15 mL
Garlic cloves, minced (or 1/2 tsp., 2 mL, powder)	2	2
Dried crushed chilies	1 tsp.	5 mL
Liquid honey	1 tsp.	5 mL
Salt	1 tsp.	5 mL
Pepper	1/2 tsp.	2 mL
Yellow cornmeal	2 tbsp.	30 mL

To butterfly roast, cut horizontally lengthwise almost, but not quite through, to other side. Open flat. Place between 2 sheets of plastic wrap. Pound with mallet or rolling pin to 1 inch (2.5 cm) thickness.

Combine next 10 ingredients in small bowl. Spread half over cut side of roast. Roll up tightly, jelly-roll style, starting from long edge. Tie with butcher's string. Spread remaining olive oil mixture over roast.

Sprinkle with cornmeal. Place, seam-side down, on greased wire rack set in medium roasting pan. Cook, uncovered, in 400°F (205°C) oven for about 30 minutes until starting to brown. Reduce heat to 325°F (160°C). Cook for about 45 minutes until internal temperature reaches 155°F (68°C). Transfer to cutting board. Cover with foil. Let stand for 10 minutes. Internal temperature of pork should rise to at least 160°F (71°C). Remove and discard butcher's string. Slice thinly. Serves 8.

1 serving: 290 Calories; 18.0 g Total Fat (9.0 g Mono, 2.0 g Poly, 5.0 g Sat); 90 mg Cholesterol; 3 g Carbohydrate; 0 g Fibre; 29 g Protein; 320 mg Sodium

Fennel Orange Lamb Shanks

It's a simple fact that lamb shanks take time to cook, though there's no doubt that good things come to those who wait. The fork-tender lamb is simply divine. Serve the sauce over pasta.

Olive oil	1 tbsp.	15 mL
Lamb shanks (about 3 – 4 lbs., 1.4 – 1.8 kg), trimmed of fat (see Note)	6	6
Salt	1/4 tsp.	1 mL
Pepper	1/4 tsp.	1 mL
Chopped onion	2 cups	500 mL
Garlic cloves, minced (or 1/2 tsp., 2 mL, powder)	2	2
Fennel seed, crushed (see Tip, page 85)	1 1/2 tsp.	7 mL
Prepared chicken broth	2 1/2 cups	625 mL
Dry (or alcohol-free) white wine	1/2 cup	125 mL
Orange juice	1/2 cup	125 mL
Tomato paste (see Tip, page 28)	1 tbsp.	15 mL
Chopped fresh parsley	2 tbsp.	30 mL
Grated orange zest (see Tip, page 94)	1 tsp.	5 mL

Heat olive oil in large frying pan on medium-high. Sprinkle lamb with salt and pepper. Cook lamb in 2 batches for about 8 minutes per batch, turning occasionally, until browned on all sides. Transfer to greased medium roasting pan. Reduce heat to medium.

Add next 3 ingredients to same frying pan. Cook for about 8 minutes, stirring often, until onion starts to brown.

Add next 4 ingredients. Heat and stir, scraping any brown bits from bottom of pan, until boiling. Pour over lamb. Cook, covered, in 350°F (175°C) oven for about 3 hours until lamb is tender. Remove lamb to serving plate. Cover to keep warm. Skim and discard fat from cooking liquid. Carefully process with hand blender, or in blender in batches, until smooth (see Safety Tip). Pour over lamb.

Sprinkle with parsley and orange zest. Serves 6.

1 serving: 350 Calories; 10.0 g Total Fat (4.5 g Mono, 1.0 g Poly, 3.5 g Sat); 150 mg Cholesterol; 11 g Carbohydrate; 1 g Fibre; 48 g Protein; 437 mg Sodium

(continued on next page)

Note: Lamb shanks are commonly found in frozen bulk packages. If using frozen shanks, remember to thaw them before using.

Safety Tip: Follow manufacturer's instructions for processing hot liquids.

Tomato Olive Pork Patties

It's about time that burgers had an uptown makeover. These Italian patties are best served in toasted ciabatta buns with provolone cheese, lettuce, fresh basil and mayo.

Large egg, fork-beaten	1	1
Fine dry bread crumbs	1/2 cup	125 mL
Finely chopped green olives	1/4 cup	60 mL
Finely chopped onion	1/4 cup	60 mL
Finely chopped sun-dried tomatoes in oil, blotted dry	1/4 cup	60 mL
Garlic clove, minced (or 1/4 tsp., 1 mL, powder)	1	1
Dried crushed chilies	1/2 tsp.	2 mL
Granulated sugar	1/2 tsp.	2 mL
Salt	1/2 tsp.	2 mL
Pepper	1/4 tsp.	1 mL
Lean ground pork	1 lb.	454 g

Combine first 10 ingredients in large bowl.

Add pork. Mix well. Divide into 4 equal portions. Shape into 4 inch (10 cm) patties. Preheat gas barbecue to medium. Place patties on greased grill. Close lid. Cook patties for about 8 minutes per side until internal temperature reaches 160°F (71°C). Makes 4 patties.

1 patty: 210 Calories; 12.0 g Total Fat (2.5 g Mono, 0.5 g Poly, 3.5 g Sat); 65 mg Cholesterol; 14 g Carbohydrate; 2 g Fibre; 11 g Protein; 570 mg Sodium

 To crush fennel seed, place in large resealable freezer bag. Seal bag. Gently hit with flat side of meat mallet or with rolling pin.

Spicy Sausage Polenta Hash

This is definitely a departure from your usual hash recipe. We've forgone the potatoes in favour of polenta, a popular staple in Italian cuisine. Add a sprinkle of grated Asiago cheese for a nice finish.

Olive oil	1 tsp.	5 mL
Hot Italian sausage, casing removed	3/4 lb.	340 g
Chopped fennel bulb (white part only)	1 1/2 cups	375 mL
Chopped red pepper	1 1/2 cups	375 mL
Chopped onion	1 cup	250 mL
Dried thyme	1/4 tsp.	1 mL
Polenta roll, sliced 1/2 inch (12 mm) thick and slices quartered	1.1 lbs.	500 g
Chopped fresh parsley	2 tbsp.	30 mL

Heat olive oil in large frying pan on medium-high. Add sausage. Scramble-fry for about 5 minutes until no longer pink. Drain.

Add next 4 ingredients. Cook for about 10 minutes, stirring often, until fennel is softened.

Add polenta. Stir. Cook, covered, for about 5 minutes, stirring occasionally, until heated through.

Sprinkle with parsley. Makes about 6 cups (1.5 L).

1 cup (250 mL): 280 Calories; 17.0 g Total Fat (0 g Mono, 0 g Poly, 6.0 g Sat); 45 mg Cholesterol; 20 g Carbohydrate; 3 g Fibre; 12 g Protein; 810 mg Sodium

Pictured on page 89.

 fyi The Italian favourite of polenta had rather humble beginnings. Maize was originally used to feed livestock until it was discovered that it could be ground into flour and used to make polenta. Polenta is extremely versatile: it can be served like porridge, or in a more dry form that can be cut or sliced.

Prosciutto-Wrapped Tenderloin

Bacon seems so commonplace when you can have prosciutto instead.
This recipe wraps pork tenderloin in a salty blanket of prosciutto ham.
Deliciously simple, moist and flavourful: pure perfection.

Olive oil	2 tsp.	10 mL
Chopped fresh basil (or 1/4 tsp., 1 mL, dried)	1 tsp.	5 mL
Chopped fresh oregano (or 1/4 tsp., 1 mL, dried)	1 tsp.	5 mL
Chopped fresh thyme (or 1/4 tsp., 1 mL, dried)	1 tsp.	5 mL
Chopped fresh rosemary (or 1/8 tsp., 0.5 mL, dried, crushed)	1/2 tsp.	2 mL
Garlic clove, minced (or 1/4 tsp., 1 mL, powder)	1	1
Pork tenderloin, trimmed of fat	1 lb.	454 g
Prosciutto (or deli) ham	3 oz.	85 g
Olive oil	1 tsp.	5 mL
Coarsely ground pepper	1/2 tsp.	2 mL

Combine first 6 ingredients in small cup.

Rub herb mixture over pork.

Wrap prosciutto slices around pork, slightly overlapping, to cover. Place, seam-side down, on greased wire rack set in baking sheet with sides.

Brush with second amount of olive oil. Sprinkle with pepper. Cook in 400°F (205°C) oven for about 30 minutes until internal temperature reaches 160°F (71°C). Transfer to cutting board. Cover with foil. Let stand for 5 minutes. Cuts into 8 slices.

1 slice: 110 Calories; 4.5 g Total Fat (2.0 g Mono, 0 g Poly, 1.5 g Sat); 40 mg Cholesterol; 0 g Carbohydrate; 0 g Fibre; 17 g Protein; 230 mg Sodium

Pictured on page 89.

Baked Ham and Pea Risotto

Rich and satisfying with classic risotto flavours and texture. This recipe comes with a teeny bit of a cheat—it's made in the oven instead of on the stovetop, which makes for a very convenient meal option.

Prepared chicken broth	2 3/4 cups	675 mL
Chopped cooked ham	1 1/2 cups	375 mL
Arborio rice	1 cup	250 mL
Frozen peas, thawed	1 1/2 cups	375 mL
Grated Parmesan cheese	1/4 cup	60 mL
White wine vinegar	1 tbsp.	15 mL

Bring broth to a boil in small saucepan. Remove from heat.

Combine ham and rice in greased shallow 2 quart (2 L) casserole. Add broth. Stir. Cook, covered, in 400°F (205°C) oven for about 35 minutes until rice is tender and liquid is almost absorbed.

Add remaining 3 ingredients. Stir. Let stand, covered, for 5 minutes. Makes about 5 1/2 cups (1.4 L).

1 cup (250 mL): 240 Calories; 4.5 g Total Fat (2.0 g Mono, 0.5 g Poly, 2.0 g Sat); 25 mg Cholesterol; 33 g Carbohydrate; 2 g Fibre; 15 g Protein; 970 mg Sodium

Pictured at right.

1. Baked Ham and Pea Risotto, above
2. Spicy Sausage Polenta Hash, page 86
3. Rosemary Asiago Risotto, page 134
4. Prosciutto-Wrapped Tenderloin, page 87

Props: Cherison Enterprises

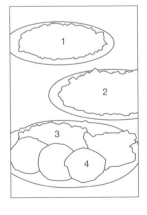

Balsamic Herb Lamb Rack

*This rack of lamb is simply decadent. Using a few basic Italian ingredients
and a simple barbecue method yields marvellous results.*

Racks of lamb (7 – 8 ribs each), about 1 lb., 454 g, each	2	2
Basil pesto	3 tbsp.	50 mL
Balsamic vinegar	1 tbsp.	15 mL
Chopped fresh rosemary (or 1/4 tsp., 1 mL, dried, crushed)	1 tsp.	5 mL
Chopped fresh thyme (or 1/4 tsp., 1 mL, dried)	1 tsp.	5 mL
Pepper	1/4 tsp.	1 mL

Preheat barbecue to medium. Place racks, bone-side up, on greased grill.
Close lid. Cook for about 2 minutes until starting to brown. Remove racks
and place bone-side down on sheet of heavy-duty (or double layer of
regular) foil.

Combine remaining 5 ingredients in small bowl. Brush over lamb. Place
racks, with foil, on grill. Close lid. Cook for about 20 minutes until internal
temperature reaches 145°F (63°C) for medium-rare or until lamb reaches
desired doneness. Transfer to cutting board. Cover with foil. Let stand for
10 minutes. Cut into 2-bone portions. Makes about eight 2-bone portions.

*One 2-bone portion: 220 Calories; 14.0 g Total Fat (3.5 g Mono, 0 g Poly, 6.0 g Sat);
95 mg Cholesterol; 2 g Carbohydrate; 0 g Fibre; 23 g Protein; 125 mg Sodium*

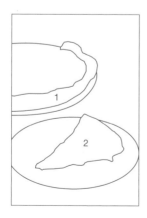

1. Whole-Wheat Pizza Crust, page 41
2. Pizza Margherita, page 95

Lamb Meatballs 'n' Sauce

Add some interest to your meal by trading up ordinary beef meatballs in favour of lamb. The thick tomato sauce makes this perfect for serving over rice or roast potatoes.

Fine dry bread crumbs	1/2 cup	125 mL
Finely chopped onion	1/2 cup	125 mL
Garlic powder	1/2 tsp.	2 mL
Salt	1/2 tsp.	2 mL
Pepper	1/2 tsp.	2 mL
Lean ground lamb	1 lb.	454 g
Olive oil	1 tsp.	5 mL
Finely chopped onion	1/2 cup	125 mL
Can of tomato sauce	14 oz.	398 mL
Bacon bits	1 tbsp.	15 mL
Balsamic vinegar	1 tbsp.	15 mL
Granulated sugar	1 tbsp.	15 mL
Dried rosemary, crushed	1 tsp.	5 mL
Dried thyme	1 tsp.	5 mL
Pepper	1/4 tsp.	1 mL

Combine first 5 ingredients in medium bowl.

Add lamb. Mix well. Roll into balls, using 1 tbsp. (15 mL) for each. Arrange in single layer on greased baking sheet with sides. Cook in 400°F (205°C) oven for about 15 minutes until no longer pink inside. Makes about 35 meatballs.

Heat olive oil in large frying pan on medium. Add onion. Cook for about 5 minutes, stirring often, until onion is softened.

Add remaining 7 ingredients. Stir. Bring to a boil. Reduce heat to medium-low. Simmer, covered, for 5 minutes to blend flavours. Add meatballs. Stir. Serves 4.

1 serving: 390 Calories; 21.0 g Total Fat (1.0 g Mono, 1.0 g Poly, 11.0 g Sat); 85 mg Cholesterol; 28 g Carbohydrate; 3 g Fibre; 23 g Protein; 968 mg Sodium

Artichoke Pork Stew

Tangy artichoke really comes through in this thick, savoury stew. Potatoes, pork and mushrooms add not only flavour but also a satisfying feel. Serve with salad and crusty bread to make it a complete meal.

Olive oil	1 tsp.	5 mL
Boneless pork shoulder blade roast, trimmed of fat and cut into 1 inch (2.5 cm) pieces	2 lbs.	900 g
Olive oil	2 tsp.	10 mL
Chopped fresh brown (or white) mushrooms	2 cups	500 mL
Chopped leek (white part only)	2 cups	500 mL
Garlic cloves, minced (or 1/2 tsp., 2 mL, powder)	2	2
Dried oregano	1 tsp.	5 mL
All-purpose flour	2 tbsp.	30 mL
Prepared vegetable broth	3 cups	750 mL
Chopped peeled potato	2 cups	500 mL
Jar of marinated artichoke hearts, drained and chopped	6 oz.	170 mL
Salt	1/2 tsp.	2 mL
Pepper	1/2 tsp.	2 mL
Lemon juice	1 tbsp.	15 mL

Heat first amount of olive oil in Dutch oven on medium-high. Add pork. Cook for about 4 minutes, stirring occasionally, until browned. Transfer to bowl. Reduce heat to medium.

Heat second amount of olive oil in same pot. Add next 4 ingredients. Cook for about 10 minutes, stirring occasionally, until mushrooms are browned.

Sprinkle with flour. Heat and stir for 1 minute. Slowly add broth, stirring constantly. Heat and stir, scraping any brown bits from bottom of pan, until boiling and thickened.

Add next 4 ingredients and pork. Stir. Cook, covered, in 350°F (175°C) oven for about 2 hours until pork is tender.

Add lemon juice. Stir. Makes about 6 cups (1.5 L).

1 cup (250 mL): 270 Calories; 9.0 g Total Fat (4.5 g Mono, 1.0 g Poly, 2.5 g Sat); 70 mg Cholesterol; 19 g Carbohydrate; 3 g Fibre; 27 g Protein; 580 mg Sodium

Creamy Lemon Pork With Capers

Pork medallions topped with capers and onion sit in a plentiful, creamy sauce. This dish features classic Italian flavours in a popular form—and there's no shortage of sauce for serving over pasta.

All-purpose flour	2 tbsp.	30 mL
Salt	1/4 tsp.	1 mL
Pepper	1/8 tsp.	0.5 mL
Pork tenderloin, trimmed of fat and cut crosswise into 8 pieces	1 lb.	454 g
Olive oil	2 tsp.	10 mL
Finely chopped onion	1/4 cup	60 mL
Prepared chicken broth	2/3 cup	150 mL
Lemon juice	2 tsp.	10 mL
Whipping cream	1/2 cup	125 mL
Capers	2 tbsp.	30 mL
Grated lemon zest (see Tip, below)	1/2 tsp.	2 mL

Combine first 3 ingredients in large resealable freezer bag. Add pork. Seal bag. Toss until coated. Remove pork. Discard any remaining flour mixture.

Heat olive oil in large frying pan on medium-high. Add pork. Cook for about 3 minutes per side until browned. Remove to plate. Cover to keep warm. Reduce heat to medium.

Add onion to same frying pan. Cook and stir for 1 minute. Add broth and lemon juice. Heat and stir, scraping any brown bits from bottom of pan, until boiling.

Add remaining 3 ingredients. Stir. Add pork. Cook for about 5 minutes, turning pork at halftime and stirring occasionally, until pork is no longer pink inside. Serves 4.

1 serving: 270 Calories; 15.0 g Total Fat (5.0 g Mono, 1.0 g Poly, 7.0 g Sat); 100 mg Cholesterol; 5 g Carbohydrate; 0 g Fibre; 28 g Protein; 410 mg Sodium

 tip   When a recipe calls for grated zest and juice, it's easier to grate the fruit first, then juice it. Be careful not to grate down to the pith (white part of the peel), which is bitter and best avoided.

Pizza Margherita

This pizza represents the colours of the Italian flag—green basil, red sauce and white cheese. For a more rustic appearance, trying pressing out the dough instead of rolling.

Tomato sauce	1/4 cup	60 mL
Balsamic vinegar	1 tsp.	5 mL
Whole-Wheat Pizza Crust, page 41 (see Note 1)	1	1
Regular bocconcini (fresh mozzarella), about 2 inch (5 cm) diameter, sliced 1/4 inch (6 mm) thick (see Note 2)	4	4
Salt, sprinkle		
Pepper, sprinkle		
Chopped fresh basil	2 tbsp.	30 mL

Combine tomato sauce and vinegar in small bowl.

Spread sauce mixture over unbaked crust to within 1/4 inch (6 mm) of edge.

Arrange cheese over top. Sprinkle with salt and pepper. Bake on bottom rack in 450°F (230°C) oven for about 15 minutes until crust is browned on bottom and cheese is starting to brown.

Sprinkle with basil. Let stand for 5 minutes. Cuts into 8 wedges.

1 wedge: 220 Calories; 10.0 g Total Fat (4.0 g Mono, 0.5 g Poly, 4.5 g Sat); 20 mg Cholesterol; 24 g Carbohydrate; 2 g Fibre; 9 g Protein; 440 mg Sodium

Pictured on page 90.

Note 1: A store-bought partially baked pizza crust may be used instead. Bake time should be adjusted to follow package directions.

Note 2: Use an egg slicer to get perfectly even slices of bocconcini. They can be difficult to slice because they are so soft and round.

Primavera Stir-Fry

You may not expect to find a stir-fry in Italian cuisine, but this tasty and colourful dish is loaded with Italian herbs and vegetables. Serve with rice, polenta or pasta.

Prepared vegetable broth	1/2 cup	125 mL
Chopped fresh basil (or 3/4 tsp., 4 mL, dried)	1 tbsp.	15 mL
Chopped fresh oregano (or 3/4 tsp., 4 mL, dried)	1 tbsp.	15 mL
Chopped fresh rosemary (or 1/4 tsp., 1 mL, dried, crushed)	1 tsp.	5 mL
Cornstarch	1 tsp.	5 mL
Salt	1/4 tsp.	1 mL
Pepper	1/8 tsp.	0.5 mL
Olive oil	1 tbsp.	15 mL
Sliced red onion	1/2 cup	125 mL
Sliced fennel bulb (white part only)	2 cups	500 mL
Sliced small zucchini (with peel)	2 cups	500 mL
Chopped eggplant (with peel), 1/2 inch (12 mm) pieces	1 cup	250 mL
Sliced red pepper	1 cup	250 mL
Sliced yellow pepper	1 cup	250 mL
Garlic cloves, minced (or 1/2 tsp., 2 mL, powder)	2	2
Chopped tomato	1 cup	250 mL

Combine first 7 ingredients in small bowl. Set aside.

Heat olive oil in large frying pan or wok on medium-high until very hot. Add onion. Stir-fry for 1 minute.

Add next 6 ingredients. Stir-fry for about 5 minutes until fennel is tender-crisp. Stir cornstarch mixture. Add to fennel mixture. Stir-fry for about 1 minute until boiling and thickened.

Add tomato. Stir. Makes about 5 cups (1.25 L).

1 cup (250 mL): 70 Calories; 3.0 g Total Fat (2.0 g Mono, 0 g Poly, 0 g Sat); 0 mg Cholesterol; 11 g Carbohydrate; 3 g Fibre; 2 g Protein; 180 mg Sodium

Vegetarian

Italian Beans and Rice

A lovely rice casserole that contains protein-packed beans and healthy fennel for a complete meal. Pesto and Asiago cheese add a punch of flavour.

Cans of romano beans (19 oz., 540 mL, each), rinsed and drained	2	2
Chopped fennel bulb (white part only)	1 1/2 cups	375 mL
Long-grain white rice	1 1/2 cups	375 mL
Chopped onion	3/4 cup	175 mL
Basil pesto	3 tbsp.	50 mL
Garlic clove, minced (or 1/4 tsp., 1 mL, powder)	1	1
Pepper	1/4 tsp.	1 mL
Prepared vegetable broth, heated	2 3/4 cups	675 mL
Grated Asiago cheese	1/4 cup	60 mL

Combine first 7 ingredients in large bowl. Spread evenly in greased 9 x 13 inch (23 x 33 cm) baking dish.

Add hot broth. Cover tightly with foil. Cook in 400°F (205°C) oven for about 45 minutes until rice is tender. Let stand, covered, for about 10 minutes until liquid is absorbed.

Sprinkle with cheese. Stir gently. Makes about 11 cups (2.75 L).

1 cup (250 mL): 150 Calories; 2.5 g Total Fat (0 g Mono, 0 g Poly, 0.5 g Sat); trace Cholesterol; 28 g Carbohydrate; 2 g Fibre; 4 g Protein; 380 mg Sodium

 If you're looking to add a little spring to your step, a hearty helping of primavera could help. Literally translated, *primavera* means "spring style." The term seems quite fitting when used in the culinary sense to describe a dish filled with fresh vegetables.

Butternut Risotto

If you avoid risotto recipes because of all that labour-intensive stirring, then this is just what you've been waiting for. Create a lovely squash risotto in your microwave. Low on effort and high on taste!

Olive oil	2 tsp.	10 mL
Chopped celery	1 cup	250 mL
Chopped onion	1 cup	250 mL
Garlic cloves, minced (or 1/2 tsp., 2 mL, powder)	2	2
Prepared vegetable broth	2 cups	500 mL
Arborio rice	1 cup	250 mL
Reserved juice from tomatoes	2/3 cup	150 mL
Dried sage	1/2 tsp.	2 mL
Dried thyme	1/4 tsp.	1 mL
Diced butternut squash	2 cups	500 mL
Can of diced tomatoes, drained and juice reserved	14 oz.	398 mL
Grated Parmesan cheese	1/2 cup	125 mL
Pepper	1/4 tsp.	1 mL

Combine first 4 ingredients in microwave-safe 3 quart (3 L) casserole. Microwave, covered, on high (100%) for about 5 minutes until celery is softened (see Tip, page 133).

Add next 5 ingredients. Stir. Microwave, covered, on high (100%) for 12 minutes.

Add squash. Stir. Microwave, covered, on high (100%) for about 10 minutes until rice is tender and creamy.

Add remaining 3 ingredients. Stir. Let stand, covered, for 5 minutes. Stir. Makes about 7 cups (1.75 L).

1 cup (250 mL): 180 Calories; 3.5 g Total Fat (1.5 g Mono, 0 g Poly, 1.5 g Sat); 5 mg Cholesterol; 32 g Carbohydrate; 2 g Fibre; 6 g Protein; 470 mg Sodium

Vegetarian

Portobello Parmesan Burgers

If ordinary veggie burgers have lost their lustre, give these portobello burgers a try. A portobello mushroom cap hides inside a crusty ciabatta bun, complete with Italian-themed burger fixings.

Balsamic vinegar	3 tbsp.	50 mL
Olive oil	3 tbsp.	50 mL
Granulated sugar	1/2 tsp.	2 mL
Salt	1/4 tsp.	1 mL
Pepper	1/4 tsp.	1 mL
Portobello mushrooms, stems and gills removed (see Note)	4	4
Grated Parmesan cheese	1/2 cup	125 mL
Mayonnaise	1/4 cup	60 mL
Sun-dried tomato pesto	2 tbsp.	30 mL
Finely chopped pine nuts, toasted (see Tip, page 46)	1 tbsp.	15 mL
Round ciabatta buns, split	4	4
Romaine lettuce leaves	4	4

Combine first 5 ingredients in small cup.

Place mushrooms in large resealable freezer bag. Pour vinegar mixture over top. Seal bag. Turn until coated. Marinate in refrigerator for 1 hour, turning occasionally. Remove mushrooms. Discard remaining vinegar mixture. Arrange mushrooms, stem-side down, on greased baking sheet with sides. Cook in 375°F (190°C) oven for about 10 minutes until tender. Turn mushrooms stem-side up.

Sprinkle cheese over mushrooms. Broil on top rack in oven for about 5 minutes until cheese is golden.

Combine next 3 ingredients in small bowl. Spread on bun halves.

Serve mushrooms, topped with lettuce, in buns. Makes 4 burgers.

1 burger: 470 Calories; 25.0 g Total Fat (6.0 g Mono, 2.0 g Poly, 4.5 g Sat); 10 mg Cholesterol; 48 g Carbohydrate; 4 g Fibre; 15 g Protein; 440 mg Sodium

Note: Because the gills can sometimes be bitter, be sure to remove them from the portobellos before marinating. First remove the stems, then, using a small spoon, scrape out and discard the gills.

Vegetarian

Eggplant Polenta Bake

A lovely layered dish of homemade polenta, veggies and cheese. This hearty casserole contains plenty of vegetables for a nutritious one-dish meal, and portions easily at the table.

Prepared vegetable broth	3 cups	750 mL
Yellow cornmeal	1 1/2 cups	375 mL
Chopped fresh spinach leaves, lightly packed	4 cups	1 L
Chopped eggplant (with peel), 1 inch (2.5 cm) pieces	6 cups	1.5 L
Chopped Roma (plum) tomato	4 cups	1 L
Can of tomato sauce	14 oz.	398 mL
Italian seasoning	1 tbsp.	15 mL
Garlic cloves, minced (or 1/2 tsp., 2 mL, powder)	2	2
Granulated sugar	1 tsp.	5 mL
Grated mozzarella cheese	1 cup	250 mL
Grated Parmesan cheese	1 cup	250 mL

Bring broth to a boil in medium saucepan. Slowly add cornmeal, stirring constantly. Heat and stir for about 5 minutes until mixture thickens and pulls away from side of pan.

Add spinach. Stir. Spread evenly in greased 9 x 13 inch (23 x 33 cm) baking dish.

Combine next 6 ingredients in large bowl. Spread evenly over cornmeal mixture. Bake, uncovered, in 375°F (190°C) oven for about 75 minutes until eggplant is tender.

Sprinkle with mozzarella and Parmesan cheeses. Bake for about 15 minutes until golden. Let stand for 10 minutes. Cuts into 6 pieces.

1 piece: 360 Calories; 10.0 g Total Fat (2.5 g Mono, 0.5 g Poly, 5.0 g Sat); 30 mg Cholesterol; 51 g Carbohydrate; 7 g Fibre; 17 g Protein; 1030 mg Sodium

Vegetarian

Chickpea Artichoke Bake

A pleasing casserole that boasts a warm golden colour and tangy artichoke flavour. This is one recipe that's sure to satisfy.

Olive oil	1 tsp.	5 mL
Chopped onion	1 cup	250 mL
Can of diced tomatoes, drained	28 oz.	796 mL
Can of chickpeas (garbanzo beans), rinsed and drained	19 oz.	540 mL
Can of artichoke hearts, drained and chopped	14 oz.	398 mL
Half-and-half cream	1/4 cup	60 mL
Basil pesto	2 tbsp.	30 mL
Red wine vinegar	1 tbsp.	15 mL
Garlic cloves, minced (or 1/2 tsp., 2 mL, powder)	2	2
Granulated sugar	1 tsp.	5 mL
Fine dry bread crumbs	1/2 cup	125 mL
Butter (or hard margarine), melted	2 tbsp.	30 mL

Heat olive oil in large saucepan on medium. Add onion. Cook for about 5 minutes, stirring often, until softened.

Add next 8 ingredients. Stir. Cook, uncovered, for about 5 minutes, stirring occasionally, until heated through. Transfer to greased 9 x 13 inch (23 x 33 cm) baking dish.

Combine bread crumbs and butter in small bowl. Sprinkle over top. Broil on centre rack in oven for about 5 minutes until golden. Serves 6.

1 serving: 190 Calories; 9.0 g Total Fat (2.0 g Mono, 0 g Poly, 4.0 g Sat); 15 mg Cholesterol; 25 g Carbohydrate; 5 g Fibre; 7 g Protein; 680 mg Sodium

Vegetarian

Porcini Lentil Ragù

A delicious mix of lentils, vegetables and tomato sauce. This broadly appealing dish packs just a hint of chili heat. Serve over polenta, egg noodles or your favourite pasta.

Prepared vegetable broth	1 cup	250 mL
Package of dried porcini mushrooms	3/4 oz.	22 g
Olive oil	2 tsp.	10 mL
Chopped onion	1 1/2 cups	375 mL
Finely chopped carrot	1 cup	250 mL
Finely chopped celery	1 cup	250 mL
Tomato paste (see Tip, page 28)	2 tbsp.	30 mL
Can of lentils, rinsed and drained	19 oz.	540 mL
Can of diced tomatoes (with juice)	14 oz.	398 mL
Dry (or alcohol-free) red wine	1/2 cup	125 mL
Garlic cloves, minced (or 1/2 tsp., 2 mL, powder)	2	2
Chopped fresh thyme (or 1/4 tsp., 1 mL, dried)	1 tsp.	5 mL
Dried crushed chilies	1/4 tsp.	1 mL
Salt	1/8 tsp.	0.5 mL
Pepper	1/4 tsp.	1 mL
Goat (chèvre) cheese, cut up	2 oz.	57 g

Bring broth to a boil in small saucepan. Add mushrooms. Stir. Remove from heat. Let stand, covered, for 10 minutes. Remove mushrooms to cutting board with slotted spoon. Chop. Strain broth through fine sieve into small bowl. Discard solids.

Heat olive oil in large saucepan on medium. Add next 3 ingredients. Cook for about 10 minutes, stirring often, until onion is softened.

Add tomato paste. Heat and stir for 1 minute.

Add next 8 ingredients, mushrooms and broth. Stir. Bring to a boil. Reduce heat to medium-low. Simmer, covered, for about 30 minutes until vegetables are tender.

Add cheese. Stir. Makes about 5 1/2 cups (1.4 L).

(continued on next page)

Vegetarian

Pictured on page 107.

Garlic Ceci and Chard

Ceci (pronounced CHEH-chee) is Italian for chickpeas or garbanzo beans. We've put this popular ingredient to good use in a colourful blend of vegetables, all with a heavy hit of garlic to make things really interesting.

Olive oil	2 tbsp.	30 mL
Can of chickpeas (garbanzo beans), rinsed and drained	19 oz.	540 mL
Chopped onion	1/2 cup	125 mL
Garlic cloves, chopped	4	4
Chopped Swiss chard, lightly packed	12 cups	3 L
Salt	1/2 tsp.	2 mL
Pepper	1/2 tsp.	2 mL
Prepared vegetable broth	1/2 cup	125 mL
Diced seeded tomato	1 cup	250 mL
Sliced green onion	3 tbsp.	50 mL
Grated lemon zest	1/2 tsp.	2 mL

Heat olive oil in Dutch oven on medium. Add next 3 ingredients. Cook for about 10 minutes, stirring often, until golden.

Add next 3 ingredients. Stir. Cook for about 3 minutes, stirring occasionally, until chard starts to wilt.

Add broth. Bring to a boil. Cook, covered, for about 5 minutes, stirring occasionally, until chard is tender. Remove from heat.

Add remaining 3 ingredients. Stir. Makes about 6 1/4 cups (1.5 L).

Pictured on page 107.

Saucy Polenta Bake

A saucy mix of tender veggies hides beneath a layer of golden polenta and pine nuts. The rest of the polenta roll can be used in Vegetable Polenta Stacks, page 22, or Golden Grilled Polenta, page 128.

Butter (or hard margarine)	2 tbsp.	30 mL
Chopped onion	2 cups	500 mL
Sliced carrot	1 1/2 cups	375 mL
Italian seasoning	1 1/2 tsp.	7 mL
Garlic clove, minced (or 1/4 tsp., 1 mL, powder)	1	1
All-purpose flour	3 tbsp.	50 mL
Salt	1/4 tsp.	1 mL
Pepper	1/4 tsp.	1 mL
Prepared vegetable broth	1 3/4 cups	425 mL
Chopped zucchini (with peel)	2 cups	500 mL
Fresh spinach leaves, lightly packed	2 cups	500 mL
Polenta roll (2.2 lbs., 1 kg), cut into 12 slices	1/2	1/2
Butter (or hard margarine), melted	1 tbsp.	15 mL
Pine nuts	2 tbsp.	30 mL

Melt first amount of butter in large saucepan on medium. Add next 4 ingredients. Cook for about 15 minutes, stirring often, until carrot is tender-crisp.

Add next 3 ingredients. Heat and stir for 1 minute. Slowly add broth, stirring constantly. Heat and stir until boiling and thickened. Remove from heat. Add zucchini and spinach. Stir. Transfer to greased 8 x 8 inch (20 x 20 cm) baking dish.

Arrange polenta slices, slightly overlapping, over top. Brush with second amount of butter. Scatter pine nuts over polenta. Bake, uncovered, in 350°F (175°C) oven for about 35 minutes until zucchini is tender-crisp and polenta is heated through. Let stand for 10 minutes. Serves 4.

1 serving: 280 Calories; 12.0 g Total Fat (3.0 g Mono, 2.0 g Poly, 2.0 g Sat); 25 mg Cholesterol; 39 g Carbohydrate; 5 g Fibre; 6 g Protein; 860 mg Sodium

Pictured on page 107.

Garlic Crumb Linguine

If you're looking to shake things up a bit, this lovely pasta dish will add interest to your dinner table. A golden bread crumb topping with pine nuts and capers adds just enough interest to a garlicky linguine.

Linguine	12 oz.	340 g
Olive oil	1/4 cup	60 mL
Garlic cloves, minced	4	4
Fresh bread crumbs (about 6 bread slices)	3 cups	750 mL
Pine nuts	1/2 cup	125 mL
Grated lemon zest	1 tbsp.	15 mL
Olive oil	1 tsp.	5 mL
Finely chopped onion	1 cup	250 mL
Chopped fresh parsley	1/4 cup	60 mL
Capers	3 tbsp.	50 mL
Lemon juice	3 tbsp.	50 mL
Salt	1/2 tsp.	2 mL
Coarsely ground pepper	1/2 tsp.	2 mL

Cook pasta according to package directions. Drain, reserving 1/2 cup (125 mL) cooking water. Return pasta to same pot. Cover to keep warm.

Heat first amount of olive oil in large frying pan on medium. Add garlic. Cook for about 2 minutes, stirring often, until golden. Add next 3 ingredients. Heat and stir for about 9 minutes until bread crumbs are crisp. Transfer to small bowl.

Heat second amount of olive oil in same frying pan. Add onion. Cook for about 5 minutes, stirring often, until softened. Add to pasta.

Add remaining 5 ingredients and reserved cooking water. Toss. Transfer to serving dish. Sprinkle with bread crumb mixture. Makes about 6 cups (1.5 L).

1 cup (250 mL): 470 Calories; 20.0 g Total Fat (9.0 g Mono, 5.0 g Poly, 2.0 g Sat); 0 mg Cholesterol; 64 g Carbohydrate; 3 g Fibre; 11 g Protein; 500 mg Sodium

Creamy Spinach Noodles

Though this recipe may contain a few of the family's highly contested ingredients, this tender pasta dish with a creamy sauce will have your family eating—and enjoying—spinach and blue cheese.

Broad egg noodles	3 cups	750 mL
Olive oil	1 tsp.	5 mL
Chopped onion	1 cup	250 mL
Garlic clove, minced (or 1/4 tsp., 1 mL, powder)	1	1
Alfredo pasta sauce	1 1/2 cups	375 mL
Box of frozen chopped spinach, thawed and squeezed dry	10 oz.	300 g
Chopped cooked chicken (see Tip, page 121)	1 cup	250 mL
Crumbled blue cheese	2 tbsp.	30 mL
Lemon juice	1 tbsp.	15 mL
Pepper	1/4 tsp.	1 mL

Cook noodles according to package directions. Drain, reserving 1/2 cup (125 mL) cooking water. Return noodles to same pot. Cover to keep warm.

Heat olive oil in large frying pan on medium. Add onion and garlic. Cook for about 5 minutes, stirring often, until onion is softened.

Add remaining 6 ingredients and reserved cooking water. Bring to a boil. Reduce heat to medium-low. Simmer, uncovered, for about 5 minutes, stirring occasionally, until heated through. Add noodles. Stir. Makes about 6 cups (1.5 L).

1 cup (250 mL): 250 Calories; 11.0 g Total Fat (1.5 g Mono, 1.0 g Poly, 6.0 g Sat); 65 mg Cholesterol; 23 g Carbohydrate; 2 g Fibre; 15 g Protein; 470 mg Sodium

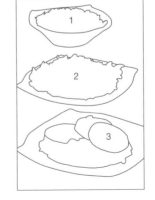

1. Garlic Ceci and Chard, page 103
2. Porcini Lentil Ragù, page 102
3. Saucy Polenta Bake, page 104

Props: Moderno

Antipasti Rotini

*An assortment of ingredients from the antipasti tray create the base for this
ingenious pasta dish. Tomato sauce binds everything together for a delicious
dish that can be made with your dinner party's antipasti leftovers.*

Rotini pasta	3 cups	750 mL
Olive oil	2 tsp.	10 mL
Chopped fennel bulb (white part only)	1 cup	250 mL
Genoa salami slices, cut into thin strips	4 oz.	113 g
Tomato pasta sauce	2 cups	500 mL
Chopped kalamata olives	1/3 cup	75 mL

Cook pasta according to package directions. Drain, reserving 1/2 cup
(125 mL) cooking water. Return pasta to same pot. Cover to keep warm.

Heat olive oil in large frying pan on medium-high. Add fennel and salami.
Cook for about 3 minutes, stirring occasionally, until fennel starts to brown.

Add pasta sauce. Stir. Reduce heat to medium-low. Simmer, covered, for
about 5 minutes until fennel is tender.

Add olives, pasta and reserved cooking water. Stir. Makes about 5 cups
(1.25 L).

*1 cup (250 mL): 340 Calories; 13.0 g Total Fat (4.5 g Mono, 0 g Poly, 2.0 g Sat); 20 mg Cholesterol;
47 g Carbohydrate; 4 g Fibre; 12 g Protein; 1210 mg Sodium*

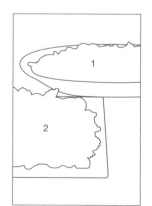

1. Salmon Artichoke Fettuccine, page 111
2. Basil Chicken Bow Ties, page 110

Basil Chicken Bow Ties

Add a touch of intrigue to your next black-tie affair. This slick little dish includes a recipe for nut-free pesto. All your allergy-sensitive dinner guests will wonder how you did it, but they're sure to thank you for it.

NUT-FREE BASIL PESTO

Fresh basil leaves, lightly packed	1 cup	250 mL
Olive oil	1/4 cup	60 mL
Garlic cloves, minced	2	2
Salt	1/4 tsp.	1 mL
Pepper	1/4 tsp.	1 mL
Grated Parmesan cheese	1/2 cup	125 mL

PASTA

Medium bow pasta	3 cups	750 mL
Olive oil	1 tsp.	5 mL
Boneless, skinless chicken breast halves, cut into 1/2 inch (12 mm) pieces	1 lb.	454 g
Salt, sprinkle		
Pepper, sprinkle		
Cherry (or grape) tomatoes, halved	2 cups	500 mL

Nut-Free Basil Pesto: Process first 5 ingredients in blender or food processor until smooth. Add cheese. Process until combined. Makes about 1/2 cup (125 mL).

Pasta: Cook pasta according to package directions. Drain, reserving 1/3 cup (75 mL) cooking water. Return pasta to same pot. Cover to keep warm.

Heat olive oil in large frying pan on medium. Add chicken. Sprinkle with salt and pepper. Cook for about 12 minutes, stirring occasionally, until chicken is no longer pink inside. Add to pasta.

Add tomatoes, Nut-Free Basil Pesto and reserved cooking water. Toss. Makes about 6 cups (1.5 L).

1 cup (250 mL): 350 Calories; 14.0 g Total Fat (8.0 g Mono, 1.5 g Poly, 3.0 g Sat); 50 mg Cholesterol; 29 g Carbohydrate; 2 g Fibre; 26 g Protein; 260 mg Sodium

Pictured on page 108.

Salmon Artichoke Fettuccine

Smoky salmon infuses a creamy sauce filled with tender artichoke hearts and wine. This easy recipe comes together quickly for those occasions where time is of the essence.

Fettuccine	8 oz.	225 g
Olive oil	1 tsp.	5 mL
Garlic cloves, minced (or 1/2 tsp., 2 mL, powder)	2	2
Can of artichoke hearts, drained and chopped	14 oz.	398 mL
Dry (or alcohol-free) white wine	1/3 cup	75 mL
Can of evaporated milk	13 oz.	370 mL
Julienned smoked salmon (see Tip, below), about 3 oz. (85 g)	1/2 cup	125 mL
Grated Romano cheese	1/4 cup	60 mL
Chopped fresh parsley	2 tbsp.	30 mL

Cook pasta according to package directions. Drain. Return to same pot. Cover to keep warm.

Heat olive oil in large frying pan on medium. Add garlic. Heat and stir for about 30 seconds until fragrant. Add artichoke hearts and wine. Simmer for about 5 minutes until wine is almost evaporated.

Add evaporated milk. Stir. Simmer for about 5 minutes, stirring often, until thickened.

Add remaining 3 ingredients and pasta. Heat and stir for about 1 minute until coated and heated through. Makes about 4 1/2 cups (1.1 L).

1 cup (250 mL): 320 Calories; 3.5 g Total Fat (1.5 g Mono, 0 g Poly, 1.0 g Sat); 10 mg Cholesterol; 50 g Carbohydrate; 3 g Fibre; 16 g Protein; 410 mg Sodium

Pictured on page 108.

 tip To julienne, cut into very thin strips that resemble matchsticks.

Wine-Sauced Pork Fettuccine

Notes of wine, garlic and cheese provide a lovely accompaniment for tender pork and pasta. A dish that's sure to have broad appeal.

Fettuccine	8 oz.	225 g
Olive oil	1 tbsp.	15 mL
Pork tenderloin, trimmed of fat, thinly sliced and cut into 3/4 inch (2 cm) wide strips	1 lb.	454 g
Olive oil	1 tsp.	5 mL
Chopped onion	1 cup	250 mL
Dijon mustard	1 tbsp.	15 mL
Garlic cloves, minced (or 3/4 tsp., 4 mL, powder)	3	3
Dry (or alcohol-free) white wine	1/2 cup	125 mL
Prepared chicken broth	1 cup	250 mL
Chopped fresh parsley	1/4 cup	60 mL
Grated Romano cheese	1/4 cup	60 mL

Cook pasta according to package directions. Drain. Return to same pot. Cover to keep warm.

Heat first amount of olive oil in large frying pan on medium-high. Add pork. Cook for about 2 minutes, stirring occasionally, until browned. Remove to large plate. Cover to keep warm. Reduce heat to medium.

Heat second amount of olive oil in same frying pan. Add onion. Cook for about 5 minutes, stirring often, until softened.

Add mustard and garlic. Heat and stir for about 1 minute until fragrant.

Add wine. Heat and stir for 2 minutes. Add broth and parsley. Stir. Bring to a boil. Add pork. Reduce heat to medium-low. Cook and stir for about 2 minutes until heated through. Add to pasta.

Sprinkle with cheese. Toss. Makes about 8 cups (2 L).

1 cup (250 mL): 230 Calories; 4.5 g Total Fat (2.5 g Mono, 0 g Poly, 1.5 g Sat); 35 mg Cholesterol; 24 g Carbohydrate; trace Fibre; 18 g Protein; 160 mg Sodium

Chickpea Fennel Shells

If you thought a dairy-free baked pasta was impossible, we've just proven you wrong. Pasta shells are always a classy dinner choice, and this version is one that everyone can enjoy.

Jumbo shell pasta	24	24
Olive oil	2 tsp.	10 mL
Chopped fennel bulb (white part only)	2 cups	500 mL
Chopped onion	1 cup	250 mL
Garlic cloves, minced (or 1/2 tsp., 2 mL, powder)	2	2
Fennel seed, crushed (see Tip, page 85)	1/2 tsp.	2 mL
Salt	1/4 tsp.	1 mL
Can of chickpeas (garbanzo beans), rinsed and drained, mashed	19 oz.	540 mL
Diced red pepper	1 cup	250 mL
Chopped green olives	1/2 cup	125 mL
Tomato pasta sauce	2 cups	500 mL
Water	1/2 cup	125 mL
Chopped fresh parsley	1 tbsp.	15 mL

Cook pasta according to package directions. Drain. Rinse with cold water. Drain well.

Heat olive oil in large frying pan on medium. Add next 5 ingredients. Cook for about 10 minutes, stirring often, until onion is softened.

Add next 3 ingredients. Stir until combined. Remove from heat.

Combine pasta sauce and second amount of water in small bowl. Spread 1/2 cup (125 mL) in bottom of ungreased 9 x 13 inch (23 x 33 cm) baking dish. Fill pasta shells with chickpea mixture. Arrange in single layer over sauce mixture in baking dish. Drizzle with remaining sauce mixture. Bake, covered, in 350°F (175°C) oven for about 40 minutes until heated through.

Sprinkle with parsley. Makes 24 stuffed shells. Serves 6.

1 serving: 240 Calories; 4.5 g Total Fat (2.0 g Mono, 0 g Poly, 0 g Sat); 0 mg Cholesterol; 46 g Carbohydrate; 7 g Fibre; 9 g Protein; 700 mg Sodium

Veggie Ball Spaghetti

Spaghetti and meatballs, just without the meat! Everyone will enjoy these tender meatless bites. For variety, try them with a mushroom or Alfredo sauce.

Olive oil	1 tsp.	5 mL
Finely chopped celery	1/2 cup	125 mL
Finely chopped onion	1/2 cup	125 mL
Garlic cloves, minced (or 1/2 tsp., 2 mL, powder)	2	2
Prepared vegetable broth	3/4 cup	175 mL
Finely chopped red pepper	1/2 cup	125 mL
Seasoned salt	1/2 tsp.	2 mL
Pepper	1/4 tsp.	1 mL
Bulgur	1/3 cup	75 mL
Fine dry bread crumbs	1/4 cup	60 mL
Large egg, fork-beaten	1	1
Olive oil	2 tsp.	10 mL
Tomato pasta sauce	2 2/3 cups	650 mL
Spaghetti	10 oz.	285 g
Grated Parmesan cheese	1/4 cup	60 mL

Heat first amount of olive oil in large frying pan on medium. Add next 3 ingredients. Cook for about 5 minutes, stirring occasionally, until onion is softened.

Add next 4 ingredients. Bring to a boil. Add bulgur. Boil, uncovered, for about 5 minutes until bulgur is tender and liquid is absorbed. Remove from heat. Transfer to medium bowl. Let stand for 5 minutes.

Add bread crumbs. Stir until combined. Add egg. Stir. Form into 1 inch (2.5 cm) balls. Makes about 28 veggie balls.

Heat second amount of olive oil in large frying pan on medium. Add veggie balls. Cook for about 10 minutes, turning occasionally, until browned. Add pasta sauce. Stir gently. Bring to a boil. Reduce heat to medium-low. Simmer, covered, for about 2 minutes until heated through.

Cook pasta according to package directions. Drain. Add to veggie ball mixture. Toss until coated. Transfer to serving bowl.

(continued on next page)

Sprinkle with cheese. Makes about 8 cups (2 L).

1 cup (250 mL): 240 Calories; 4.5 g Total Fat (2.0 g Mono, 0.5 g Poly, 1.0 g Sat); 20 mg Cholesterol; 43 g Carbohydrate; 5 g Fibre; 9 g Protein; 610 mg Sodium

Lazy Meatball Rigatoni

If you love meatballs but find making them a bit too labour-intensive, this recipe provides a great solution. Simply cut Italian sausage into slices without removing the casing and cook them up. Presto! You've got meatballs in minutes.

Olive oil	1 tsp.	5 mL
Hot (or mild) Italian sausage, cut into 1 inch (2.5 cm) slices	1 lb.	454 g
Quartered fresh white mushrooms	2 cups	500 mL
Chopped onion	1 cup	250 mL
Garlic cloves, minced (or 1/2 tsp., 2 mL, powder)	2	2
Fennel seed	1/4 tsp.	1 mL
Tomato pasta sauce	2 1/2 cups	625 mL
Water	1/2 cup	125 mL
Balsamic vinegar	1 tbsp.	15 mL
Rigatoni pasta	3 1/2 cups	875 mL

Heat olive oil in large frying pan on medium-high. Add sausage. Cook for about 5 minutes, stirring occasionally, until browned. Remove with slotted spoon to plate. Cover to keep warm. Drain and discard all but 1 tsp. (5 mL) drippings. Reduce heat to medium.

Add next 4 ingredients to same frying pan. Cook for about 8 minutes, stirring often, until onion is softened.

Add next 3 ingredients and sausage. Stir. Reduce heat to medium-low. Simmer, covered, for about 15 minutes until sausage is no longer pink inside.

Cook pasta according to package directions. Drain. Add to sausage mixture. Stir. Makes about 8 cups (2 L).

1 cup (250 mL): 350 Calories; 19.0 g Total Fat (0.5 g Mono, 0 g Poly, 6.0 g Sat); 45 mg Cholesterol; 31 g Carbohydrate; 3 g Fibre; 14 g Protein; 890 mg Sodium

Beef Tortellini Bake

This easy recipe will keep the cook happy—and the simple Italian flavours will leave the family content!

Fresh beef-filled tortellini	4 cups	1 L
Sliced fresh white mushrooms	3 cups	750 mL
Tomato pasta sauce	3 cups	750 mL
Water	1 cup	250 mL
Dried oregano	1 tsp.	5 mL
Grated Italian cheese blend	1 cup	250 mL

Combine first 5 ingredients in large bowl. Transfer to greased 3 quart (3 L) casserole. Bake, covered, in 350°F (175°C) oven for about 1 hour until tortellini is tender and edges are bubbling.

Sprinkle with cheese. Let stand, covered, for about 5 minutes until cheese is melted. Makes about 9 cups (2.25 L).

1 cup (250 mL): 220 Calories; 7.0 g Total Fat (0 g Mono, 0 g Poly, 3.0 g Sat); 20 mg Cholesterol; 30 g Carbohydrate; 3 g Fibre; 9 g Protein; 690 mg Sodium

Leek and Clam Spaghettini

Everyone will be clamouring for more of this tomato pasta with clams, leek and feta—and all in an impressive recipe that takes very little time to put together.

Olive oil	1 tsp.	5 mL
Sliced leek (white part only)	2 cups	500 mL
Can of diced tomatoes, drained	14 oz.	398 mL
Can of tomato sauce	14 oz.	398 mL
Garlic cloves, minced (or 1/2 tsp., 2 mL, powder)	2	2
Can of whole baby clams (with liquid)	5 oz.	142 g
Spaghettini	8 oz.	225 g
Crumbled feta cheese	1/4 cup	60 mL

Heat olive oil in medium saucepan on medium. Add leek. Cook, uncovered, for about 5 minutes, stirring occasionally, until softened.

(continued on next page)

Add next 3 ingredients. Stir. Bring to a boil. Reduce heat to medium-low. Simmer, uncovered, for 10 minutes to blend flavours.

Add clams with liquid. Cook and stir until heated through.

Cook pasta according to package directions. Drain. Return to same pot.

Add cheese and clam mixture. Toss. Makes about 7 cups (1.75 L).

1 cup (250 mL): 190 Calories; 2.5 g Total Fat (1.0 g Mono, 0 g Poly, 1.0 g Sat); 5 mg Cholesterol; 35 g Carbohydrate; 3 g Fibre; 7 g Protein; 590 mg Sodium

---

Marco Polo Noodles

There'll be no searching for flavour here. Marco Polo would certainly approve of this pasta dish with a Venetian flair.

Olive oil	1 tsp.	5 mL
Chopped onion	1/2 cup	125 mL
Garlic clove, minced (or 1/4 tsp., 1 mL, powder)	1	1
Salt	1/4 tsp.	1 mL
Pepper	1/4 tsp.	1 mL
Small bay scallops	3/4 lb.	340 g
Can of romano beans, rinsed and drained	19 oz.	540 mL
Frozen peas, thawed	1 cup	250 mL
Broad egg noodles	3 cups	750 mL
Chopped fresh parsley	1/4 cup	60 mL
Lemon juice	1 tbsp.	15 mL

Heat olive oil in large frying pan on medium. Add next 4 ingredients. Cook for about 5 minutes, stirring often, until onion is softened.

Add next 3 ingredients. Cook for about 5 minutes, stirring occasionally, until scallops are opaque.

Cook noodles according to package directions. Drain, reserving 1/4 cup (60 mL) cooking water. Return noodles to same pot.

Add parsley, lemon juice and scallop mixture. Toss, adding reserved cooking water 2 tbsp. (30 mL) at a time, if necessary, to moisten. Makes about 6 cups (1.5 L).

1 cup (250 mL): 230 Calories; 2.5 g Total Fat (1.0 g Mono, 0.5 g Poly, 0 g Sat); 35 mg Cholesterol; 34 g Carbohydrate; 8 g Fibre; 19 g Protein; 340 mg Sodium

Creamy Vegetable Lasagna

Cream-sauced pastas need not lead to feelings of guilt. This cheesy, saucy dish contains a hearty helping of vegetables for a boost of both flavour and nutrition.

Olive oil	1 tbsp.	15 mL
Chopped onion	2 cups	500 mL
Sliced fresh white mushrooms	2 cups	500 mL
Sliced celery	1 cup	250 mL
Chopped zucchini (with peel)	2 cups	500 mL
Frozen tiny peas	1 cup	250 mL
Basil pesto	1/4 cup	60 mL
Alfredo pasta sauce	2 1/2 cups	625 mL
Dry (or alcohol-free) white wine	1/2 cup	125 mL
Water	1/2 cup	125 mL
Oven-ready lasagna noodles	12	12
Grated mozzarella cheese	2 cups	500 mL

Heat olive oil in large frying pan on medium-high. Add next 3 ingredients. Cook for about 10 minutes, stirring often, until celery starts to soften. Reduce heat to medium.

Add zucchini. Cook for about 5 minutes, stirring occasionally, until celery is softened. Add peas and pesto. Stir.

Combine next 3 ingredients in medium bowl.

To assemble, layer ingredients in greased 9 x 13 inch (23 x 33 cm) baking dish as follows:

1. 1 cup (250 mL) sauce mixture
2. 4 noodles
3. Half of mushroom mixture
5. 1 cup (250 mL) sauce mixture
6. 4 noodles
7. Remaining mushroom mixture
8. Remaining 4 noodles
9. Remaining sauce mixture

(continued on next page)

Sprinkle with cheese. Cover with greased foil. Bake in 350°F (175°C) oven for about 50 minutes until noodles are tender. Carefully remove foil. Bake for another 20 minutes until cheese is golden. Let stand for 10 minutes. Cuts into 8 pieces.

1 piece: 397 Calories; 21.0 g Total Fat (3.0 g Mono, 1.0 g Poly, 10.0 g Sat); 55 mg Cholesterol; 34 g Carbohydrate; 3 g Fibre; 17 g Protein; 590 mg Sodium

Skillet Lasagna

If your family loves lasagna but you can't quite seem to fit all that cooking and baking time into your busy schedule, this recipe is sure to tame the craving. Comes together quickly once you're home from the office.

Olive oil	1 tsp.	5 mL
Lean ground beef	1 lb.	454 g
Chopped onion	1 cup	250 mL
Garlic clove, minced (or 1/4 tsp., 1 mL, powder)	1	1
Italian seasoning	1 tsp.	5 mL
Dried crushed chilies	1/4 tsp.	1 mL
Boiling water	2 cups	500 mL
Can of diced tomatoes (with juice)	14 oz.	398 mL
Alfredo pasta sauce	1 cup	250 mL
Tomato paste (see Tip, page 28)	3 tbsp.	50 mL
Oven-ready lasagna noodles, broken into 4 pieces each	8	8
Grated mozzarella cheese	1/2 cup	125 mL

Heat olive oil in large frying pan on medium-high. Add next 5 ingredients. Scramble-fry for about 8 minutes until onion is softened.

Add next 4 ingredients. Stir. Bring to a boil.

Add noodles. Stir. Reduce heat to medium. Boil gently, covered, for about 10 minutes, stirring occasionally, until noodles are tender but firm. Remove from heat.

Sprinkle with cheese. Let stand, covered, for about 2 minutes until cheese is melted. Serves 4.

1 serving: 470 Calories; 18.0 g Total Fat (4.0 g Mono, 0.5 g Poly, 9.0 g Sat); 120 mg Cholesterol; 41 g Carbohydrate; 3 g Fibre; 37 g Protein; 760 mg Sodium

Spaghetti Arcobaleno

This dish features an attractive arcobaleno *(Italian for "rainbow") of fresh ingredients in a delicious light sauce. Garnish with shaved Parmesan cheese and small basil leaves.*

Spaghetti	8 oz.	225 g
Olive oil	1 tsp.	5 mL
Salmon fillets, skin and any small bones removed	1 lb.	454 g
Halved grape tomatoes	2 cups	500 mL
Chopped yellow pepper	1 1/2 cups	375 mL
Whole pitted kalamata olives	1 cup	250 mL
Dry (or alcohol-free) white wine	1/2 cup	125 mL
Sun-dried tomato pesto	1/2 cup	125 mL
Salt	1/4 tsp.	1 mL
Chopped fresh asparagus (1 inch, 2.5 cm, pieces)	2 cups	500 mL
Coarsely chopped fresh basil (or 2 tbsp., 30 mL, dried)	1/2 cup	125 mL
Lemon juice	1 tbsp.	30 mL
Grated lemon zest (see Tip, page 94)	1 tsp.	5 mL
Pepper	1/4 tsp.	1 mL

Cook pasta according to package directions. Drain.

Heat olive oil in large frying pan on medium. Add fillets. Cook for about 4 minutes per side until fish flakes easily when tested with fork. Transfer to plate. Cover to keep warm.

Add next 6 ingredients to same frying pan. Bring to a boil. Cook for about 10 minutes, stirring occasionally, until yellow pepper is tender.

Add asparagus and pasta. Stir. Cook, covered, for about 1 minute until asparagus is tender-crisp. Transfer to large serving bowl. Break up salmon pieces. Add to pasta mixture.

Add remaining 4 ingredients. Toss. Makes about 8 1/2 cups (2.1 L).

1 cup (250 mL): 290 Calories; 12.0 g Total Fat (4.0 g Mono, 1.5 g Poly, 1.5 g Sat); 30 mg Cholesterol; 27 g Carbohydrate; 3 g Fibre; 16 g Protein; 449 mg Sodium

Pictured on front cover.

Speedy Chicken Carbonara

Rather than turning to commercially produced high-salt sauces, this recipe teaches the true method for making a carbonara sauce from scratch—and a touch of chili heat adds a dash of adventure.

Spaghetti	12 oz.	340 g
Egg yolks (large)	4	4
Grated Parmesan cheese	1/2 cup	125 mL
Finely chopped fresh parsley	1/4 cup	60 mL
Chili paste (sambal oelek)	1/2 tsp.	2 mL
Bacon slices, chopped	6	6
Chopped cooked chicken (see Tip, below)	1 1/2 cups	375 mL
Prepared chicken broth, heated	1 cup	250 mL

Cook pasta according to package directions. Drain. Return to same pot. Cover to keep warm.

Combine next 4 ingredients in small bowl. Set aside.

Cook bacon in large frying pan on medium until crisp. Remove with slotted spoon to paper towel-lined plate to drain. Drain and discard all but 1 tbsp. (15 mL) drippings.

Add chicken and pasta to same frying pan. Reduce heat to medium-low. Cook and stir for about 2 minutes until heated through.

Whisk hot broth into egg mixture. Add to pasta mixture. Add bacon. Toss until coated. Serve immediately. Makes about 6 cups (1.5 L).

1 cup (250 mL): 420 Calories; 14.0 g Total Fat (6.0 g Mono, 2.0 g Poly, 5.0 g Sat); 190 mg Cholesterol; 44 g Carbohydrate; 2 g Fibre; 26 g Protein; 350 mg Sodium

 tip Don't have any leftover chicken? Start with 2 boneless, skinless chicken breast halves (4 – 6 oz., 113 – 170 g, each). Place in large frying pan with 1 cup (250 mL) water or chicken broth. Simmer, covered, for 12 to 14 minutes until no longer pink inside. Drain. Chop. Makes about 2 cups (500 mL) cooked chicken.

Sage Chicken Ravioli

Wonton wrappers provide a much-appreciated shortcut in making homemade ravioli. A light butter and pine nut topping adds the perfect finishing touch.

Finely chopped green onion	2 tbsp.	30 mL
Finely chopped red pepper	2 tbsp.	30 mL
Chopped fresh sage (or 1/4 tsp., 1 mL, dried)	1 tsp.	5 mL
Garlic powder	1/8 tsp.	0.5 mL
Salt	1/4 tsp.	1 mL
Pepper	1/8 tsp.	0.5 mL
Lean ground chicken thigh	3/4 lb.	340 g
Wonton wrappers	48	48
Large egg	1	1
Water	1 tbsp.	15 mL
Water	12 cups	3 L
Salt	1 1/2 tsp.	7 mL
Butter (or hard margarine)	1/4 cup	60 mL
Pine nuts	1/4 cup	60 mL
Grated Parmesan cheese	2 tbsp.	30 mL
Chopped fresh sage (or 3/4 tsp., 4 mL, dried)	1 tbsp.	15 mL
Grated lemon zest	1/2 tsp.	2 mL

Combine first 6 ingredients in medium bowl. Add chicken. Mix well.

Arrange 24 wrappers on work surface. Place about 1 tbsp. (15 mL) chicken mixture in centre of each wrapper.

Whisk egg and water in small bowl. Brush over edges of wrappers. Cover with remaining wrappers. Press edges to seal. Makes 24 ravioli.

Combine water and salt in Dutch oven. Bring to a boil. Add half of ravioli. Boil, uncovered, for about 5 minutes, stirring occasionally, until chicken mixture is no longer pink and wrappers are tender but firm. Transfer with slotted spoon to sieve. Drain. Transfer to serving bowl. Cover to keep warm. Repeat with remaining ravioli.

Melt butter in small frying pan on medium. Add pine nuts. Heat and stir for about 1 minute until nuts are browned. Add remaining 3 ingredients. Stir. Pour over ravioli. Stir gently until coated. Serves 4.

(continued on next page)

1 serving: 480 Calories; 31.0 g Total Fat (5.0 g Mono, 4.0 g Poly, 9.0 g Sat); 135 mg Cholesterol; 27 g Carbohydrate; 1 g Fibre; 23 g Protein; 560 mg Sodium

Pictured on page 125.

Spaghetti Bolognese

This time-honoured Italian favourite appeals to all, young and old. Serve with grated Parmesan cheese to complete the experience.

Bacon slices, chopped	4	4
Lean ground beef	1 lb.	454 g
Finely chopped carrot	1/2 cup	125 mL
Finely chopped celery	1/2 cup	125 mL
Finely chopped onion	1/2 cup	125 mL
Garlic cloves, minced (or 1/2 tsp., 2 mL, powder)	2	2
Salt	1/2 tsp.	2 mL
Pepper	1/4 tsp.	1 mL
Tomato paste (see Tip, page 28)	1/3 cup	75 mL
Prepared beef broth	1 cup	250 mL
Dry (or alcohol-free) red wine	1/2 cup	125 mL
Half-and-half cream	1/4 cup	60 mL
Spaghetti	12 oz.	340 g

Cook bacon in large saucepan on medium until crisp. Remove with slotted spoon to paper towel-lined plate to drain. Drain and discard all but 1 tsp. (5 mL) drippings.

Add next 7 ingredients to same pot. Scramble-fry for about 10 minutes until beef is no longer pink.

Add tomato paste. Heat and stir for 1 minute. Add broth, wine and bacon. Stir. Bring to a boil. Reduce heat to medium-low. Simmer, covered, for 1 hour to blend flavours.

Add cream. Stir. Cover to keep warm.

Cook pasta according to package directions. Drain. Serve with sauce. Serves 4.

1 serving: 610 Calories; 13.0 g Total Fat (5.0 g Mono, 1.5 g Poly, 5.0 g Sat); 35 mg Cholesterol; 74 g Carbohydrate; 5 g Fibre; 41 g Protein; 660 mg Sodium

Pictured on page 125.

Broccoli and Mushroom Gnocchi

Gnocchi (pronounced NYOH-kee) are small Italian dumplings found in the pasta aisle at your grocery store. This recipe features tender gnocchi with the earthy flavours of broccoli and mushrooms, and just a hint of chili heat.

Olive oil	1 tbsp.	15 mL
Sliced fresh white mushrooms	4 cups	1 L
Chopped onion	1/2 cup	125 mL
Garlic cloves, minced (or 1/2 tsp., 2 mL, powder)	2	2
Dried crushed chilies	1/4 tsp.	1 mL
Broccoli florets	3 cups	750 mL
Prepared vegetable broth	1/2 cup	125 mL
Gnocchi	1.1 lbs.	500 g
Grated Parmesan cheese	1/4 cup	60 mL
Pepper	1/8 tsp.	0.5 mL

Heat olive oil in large frying pan on medium. Add next 4 ingredients. Cook for about 15 minutes, stirring occasionally, until mushrooms are browned and liquid is evaporated.

Add broccoli and broth. Stir. Cook, covered, for about 3 minutes until broccoli is tender-crisp. Remove from heat. Cover to keep warm.

Cook gnocchi according to package directions. Drain. Add to broccoli mixture.

Sprinkle with cheese and pepper. Toss. Makes about 5 cups (1.25 L).

1 cup (250 mL): 280 Calories; 6.0 g Total Fat (2.5 g Mono, 0.5 g Poly, 1.5 g Sat); 20 mg Cholesterol; 49 g Carbohydrate; 4 g Fibre; 11 g Protein; 690 mg Sodium

Pictured at right.

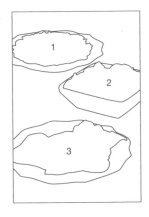

1. Spaghetti Bolognese, page 123
2. Broccoli and Mushroom Gnocchi, above
3. Sage Chicken Ravioli, page 122

Props: Casa Bugatti

Fettuccine Alfredo

This classic Alfredo recipe forgoes the use of pre-made sauces. But fear not, it's not as difficult as you might think. This dish comes together in no time and is sure to satisfy.

Fettuccine	10 oz.	285 g
Butter (or hard margarine)	1/4 cup	60 mL
Garlic clove, minced (or 1/4 tsp., 1 mL, powder)	1	1
Whipping cream	1 cup	250 mL
Grated Parmesan cheese	1/2 cup	125 mL
Salt	1/4 tsp.	1 mL
Coarsely ground pepper	1/4 tsp.	1 mL
Chopped fresh parsley (or 1/2 tsp., 2 mL, flakes)	2 tsp.	10 mL

Cook pasta according to package directions. Drain. Return pasta to same pot. Cover to keep warm.

Melt butter in small saucepan on medium. Add garlic. Heat and stir for about 1 minute until fragrant. Add whipping cream. Stir. Bring to a boil on medium. Boil gently, uncovered, for about 3 minutes, stirring occasionally, until slightly reduced. Remove from heat.

Add next 3 ingredients. Stir until cheese is melted. Add to pasta. Toss.

Sprinkle with parsley. Serve immediately. Makes about 4 1/2 cups (1.1 L).

1 cup (250 mL): 530 Calories; 32.0 g Total Fat (9.0 g Mono, 1.0 g Poly, 19.0 g Sat); 100 mg Cholesterol; 48 g Carbohydrate; 1 g Fibre; 13 g Protein; 370 mg Sodium

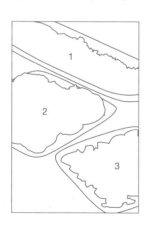

1. Golden Grilled Polenta, page 128
2. Sweet Grilled Fennel, page 128
3. Grilled Italian Veggies, page 131

Sweet Grilled Fennel

Grilling brings out the natural sweetness of fennel, with balsamic vinegar, honey and basil lending a hand. A rustic appearance makes this a great addition to a casual meal of fish, chicken, pork or veal.

Balsamic vinegar	3 tbsp.	50 mL
Olive oil	2 tbsp.	30 mL
Chopped fresh basil (or 3/4 tsp., 4 mL, dried)	1 tbsp.	15 mL
Finely chopped green onion	1 tbsp.	15 mL
Liquid honey	1 tbsp.	15 mL
Garlic clove, minced (or 1/4 tsp., 1 mL, powder)	1	1
Salt	1/4 tsp.	1 mL
Pepper	1/4 tsp.	1 mL
Medium fennel bulbs (white part only), cut into 1/2 inch (12 mm) slices	4	4

Whisk first 8 ingredients in large bowl.

Add fennel. Stir until coated. Marinate, covered, at room temperature for 30 minutes. Preheat gas barbecue to medium. Place fennel on greased grill, reserving vinegar mixture in bowl. Close lid. Cook for about 15 minutes per side until tender. Remove fennel to same bowl. Toss in vinegar mixture until coated. Makes about 5 1/2 cups (1.4 L).

1/2 cup (125 mL): 70 Calories; 2.5 g Total Fat (2.0 g Mono, 0 g Poly, 0 g Sat); 0 mg Cholesterol; 11 g Carbohydrate; 4 g Fibre; 2 g Protein; 110 mg Sodium

Pictured on page 126 and back cover.

Golden Grilled Polenta

You're good as gold when you serve this fancy side with Steak Florentine, page 55, and a glass of hearty red wine. Blue cheese may be replaced with soft goat (chèvre) cheese if you prefer. Remaining polenta can be used in Vegetable Polenta Stacks, page 22, or Saucy Polenta Bake, page 104.

Polenta roll (2.2 lbs, 1 kg), cut into 8 slices	1/2	1/2
Italian dressing	1/4 cup	60 mL

(continued on next page)

Crumbled blue cheese	1/2 cup	125 mL
Bacon slices, cooked crisp and crumbled	4	4
Coarsely chopped walnuts, toasted (see Tip, page 46)	1/4 cup	60 mL
Chopped fresh parsley	1 tbsp.	15 mL

Brush both sides of polenta slices with dressing. Preheat gas barbecue to medium. Place polenta on greased grill. Close lid. Cook for about 5 minutes per side until heated through and grill marks appear. Arrange in single layer on large serving plate.

Scatter remaining 4 ingredients, in order given, over polenta. Makes 8 slices.

1 slice: 140 Calories; 8.0 g Total Fat (1.5 g Mono, 2.0 g Poly, 2.5 g Sat); 10 mg Cholesterol; 11 g Carbohydrate; trace Fibre; 5 g Protein; 480 mg Sodium

Pictured on page 126 and back cover.

Tomato Fennel Rice Pilaf

Your microwave is your most valuable ally when it comes to fast and easy side dishes. You won't have to turn to convenience foods because this recipe provides a great side that comes together in a hurry.

Prepared chicken broth	2 3/4 cups	675 mL
Converted white rice	1 cup	250 mL
Chopped onion	1/2 cup	125 mL
Butter (or hard margarine), melted	1 tbsp.	15 mL
Tomato paste (see Tip, page 28)	1 tbsp.	15 mL
Fennel seed, crushed (see Tip, page 85)	1/2 tsp.	2 mL
Granulated sugar	1/4 tsp.	1 mL
Salt	1/4 tsp.	1 mL
Chopped seeded tomato	1/2 cup	125 mL

Combine first 8 ingredients in microwave-safe 2 quart (2 L) casserole. Microwave, covered, on high (100%) for 8 minutes (see Tip, page 133). Stir. Microwave, covered, on medium-high (70%) for about 20 minutes until rice is tender. Let stand, covered, for about 5 minutes until liquid is absorbed. Fluff with fork.

Add tomato. Stir. Makes about 4 1/2 cups (1.1 L).

1/2 cup (125 mL): 100 Calories; 1.5 g Total Fat (0 g Mono, 0 g Poly, 1.0 g Sat); trace Cholesterol; 19 g Carbohydrate; trace Fibre; 2 g Protein; 240 mg Sodium

Microwave Mushroom Polenta

If you thought polenta couldn't be made in the microwave, this recipe certainly proves you wrong. Mushrooms add an earthy tone, with pepper, garlic and cheese adding plenty of pep.

Chopped fresh white mushrooms	3 cups	750 mL
Garlic cloves, minced (or 1/2 tsp., 2 mL, powder)	2	2
Dried basil	1/2 tsp.	2 mL
Pepper	1/8 tsp.	0.5 mL
Prepared vegetable broth	3 cups	750 mL
Yellow cornmeal	1 cup	250 mL
Grated Parmesan cheese	1/3 cup	75 mL

Combine first 4 ingredients in large microwave-safe bowl. Microwave, covered, on high (100%) for about 5 minutes, stirring at halftime, until mushrooms are softened (see Tip, page 133).

Add broth and cornmeal. Stir. Microwave, covered, on high (100%) for about 10 minutes, stirring every 3 minutes, until mixture is thickened and creamy.

Stir in cheese. Makes about 4 cups (1 L).

1/2 cup (125 mL): 100 Calories; 1.5 g Total Fat (0 g Mono, 0 g Poly, 0.5 g Sat); trace Cholesterol; 19 g Carbohydrate; trace Fibre; 4 g Protein; 280 mg Sodium

Garlic Spinach

Spinach, or spinaci (pronounced spee-NAH-chee) as the Italians call it, makes a great side dish with its simple, classic flavours.

Olive oil	2 tbsp.	30 mL
Garlic clove, minced	1	1
Salt	1/8 tsp.	0.5 mL
Pepper	1/8 tsp.	0.5 mL
Fresh spinach leaves, lightly packed	10 cups	2.5 L
Lemon juice	1 tsp.	5 mL

(continued on next page)

Heat olive oil in large saucepan on medium. Add next 3 ingredients. Heat and stir for about 1 minute until garlic is fragrant.

Add spinach. Stir. Cook, covered, for about 3 minutes, stirring occasionally, until spinach is wilted.

Sprinkle with lemon juice. Stir. Makes about 2 1/2 cups (625 mL).

1/2 cup (125 mL): 60 Calories; 6.0 g Total Fat (4.0 g Mono, 0.5 g Poly, 1.0 g Sat); 0 mg Cholesterol; 2 g Carbohydrate; 1 g Fibre; 2 g Protein; 95 mg Sodium

Grilled Italian Veggies

A colourful array of vegetables hide inside each individual packet. A casual presentation for a bright and flavourful recipe.

Chopped eggplant (with peel), 1 inch (2.5 cm) pieces	2 cups	500 mL
Chopped zucchini (with peel), 1 inch (2.5 cm) pieces	2 cups	500 mL
Chopped red pepper (1 inch, 2.5 cm, pieces)	1 1/2 cups	375 mL
Chopped yellow pepper (1 inch, 2.5 cm, pieces)	1 1/2 cups	375 mL
Jars of marinated artichoke hearts, with liquid (6 oz., 170 mL, each)	2	2
Chopped onion	1 cup	250 mL
Finely chopped sun-dried tomatoes in oil	1/4 cup	60 mL
Oil from sun-dried tomatoes	1 tbsp.	15 mL
Dried oregano	1/2 tsp.	2 mL
Salt	1/4 tsp.	1 mL
Pepper	1/4 tsp.	1 mL

Stir all 11 ingredients in large bowl until coated. Cut 6 sheets of heavy-duty (or double layer of regular) foil, about 14 inches (35 cm) long. Spray 1 side with cooking spray. Spoon eggplant mixture onto greased side of foil sheets. Fold edges of foil together over vegetables to enclose. Fold ends to seal completely. Preheat gas barbecue to medium-low. Place packets, seam-side up, on ungreased grill. Close lid. Cook for about 20 minutes until vegetables are tender. Makes 6 packets.

1 packet: 80 Calories; 3.0 g Total Fat (2.0 g Mono, 0 g Poly, 0 g Sat); 0 mg Cholesterol; 13 g Carbohydrate; 4 g Fibre; 2 g Protein; 220 mg Sodium

Pictured on page 126 and back cover.

Artichoke Bean Mash

It's going to be a mash-up! This recipe is easily made in your microwave.
A perfect base for a ragout, or can simply be enjoyed alongside grilled or roast
meat dishes.

Prepared vegetable broth	1 cup	250 mL
Finely chopped onion	1/2 cup	125 mL
Garlic cloves, minced (or 1/2 tsp., 2 mL, powder)	2	2
Dried basil	1/2 tsp.	2 mL
Dried oregano	1/2 tsp.	2 mL
Salt	1/4 tsp.	1 mL
Pepper	1/4 tsp.	1 mL
Can of chickpeas (garbanzo beans), rinsed and drained	19 oz.	540 mL
Can of white kidney beans, rinsed and drained	19 oz.	540 mL
Jar of marinated artichoke hearts, drained and finely chopped	6 oz.	170 mL
Chopped fresh parsley	2 tbsp.	30 mL
Lemon juice	1 tbsp.	15 mL
Olive oil	1 tbsp.	15 mL
Grated lemon zest (see Tip, page 94)	1/2 tsp.	2 mL

Combine first 7 ingredients in microwave-safe 2 quart (2 L) casserole. Microwave, covered, on high (100%) for about 5 minutes until onion is softened (see Tip, page 133).

Add chickpeas and kidney beans. Stir. Microwave, covered, on high (100%) for about 5 minutes until heated through. Coarsely mash with potato masher.

Add remaining 5 ingredients. Stir. Makes about 4 1/2 cups (1.1 L).

1/2 cup (125 mL): 90 Calories; 2.0 g Total Fat (1.0 g Mono, 0 g Poly, 0 g Sat); 0 mg Cholesterol; 16 g Carbohydrate; 6 g Fibre; 6 g Protein; 310 mg Sodium

Prosciutto Potatoes

Stuffed potatoes are always a crowd pleaser. This version includes plenty of salty prosciutto and Romano cheese for a delightful treat that might just steal the spotlight from your main course.

Large unpeeled baking potatoes	2	2
Grated Romano cheese	1/4 cup	60 mL
Milk	1/4 cup	60 mL
Italian seasoning	1 tsp.	5 mL
Coarsely crushed seasoned croutons	1/2 cup	125 mL
Finely chopped prosciutto (or deli) ham	1/4 cup	60 mL
Grated Romano cheese	1/4 cup	60 mL

Prick potatoes in several places with fork. Wrap each potato in foil. Bake directly on centre rack in 425°F (220°C) oven for about 1 hour until tender. Transfer to cutting board. Carefully remove foil. Let stand until cool enough to handle. Cut potatoes in half lengthwise. Scoop pulp into medium bowl, leaving 1/4 inch (6 mm) shells.

Mash potato pulp with next 3 ingredients.

Add croutons and prosciutto. Stir. Spoon into shells. Place on ungreased baking sheet.

Sprinkle with second amount of cheese. Bake in 425°F (220°C) oven for about 20 minutes until heated through and starting to brown. Makes 4 stuffed potatoes.

1 stuffed potato: 260 Calories; 5.0 g Total Fat (1.5 g Mono, 0 g Poly, 2.0 g Sat); 15 mg Cholesterol; 43 g Carbohydrate; 4 g Fibre; 11 g Protein; 510 mg Sodium

 tip The microwaves used in our test kitchen are 900 watts—but microwaves are sold in many different powers. You should be able to find the wattage of yours by opening the door and looking for the mandatory label. If your microwave is more than 900 watts, you may need to reduce the cooking time. If it's less than 900 watts, you'll probably need to increase the cooking time.

Lemon Garlic Zucchini

Tender zucchini create the perfect side dish for a tomato-based main course.

Olive oil	1 tbsp.	15 mL
Sliced zucchini (with peel), about 1/2 inch (12 mm) thick	4 cups	1 L
Garlic cloves, minced (or 1/2 tsp., 2 mL, powder)	2	2
Thinly sliced green onion	1 tbsp.	15 mL
Lemon juice	2 tsp.	10 mL
Salt	1/4 tsp.	1 mL
Coarsely ground pepper	1/4 tsp.	1 mL

Heat olive oil in large frying pan on medium. Add zucchini and garlic. Cook for about 8 minutes, stirring occasionally, until zucchini starts to soften and turn brown.

Add remaining 4 ingredients. Heat and stir for 1 minute. Makes about 3 cups (750 mL).

1/2 cup (125 mL): 35 Calories; 2.5 g Total Fat (1.5 g Mono, 0 g Poly, 0 g Sat); 0 mg Cholesterol; 3 g Carbohydrate; trace Fibre; trace Protein; 85 mg Sodium

Pictured on page 71.

Rosemary Asiago Risotto

This basic version of risotto makes a great side dish for a lighter main course.

Prepared chicken broth	5 1/2 cups	1.4 L
Dried rosemary, crushed	1/2 tsp.	2 mL
Butter (or hard margarine)	2 tbsp.	30 mL
Arborio rice	1 1/2 cups	375 mL
Grated Asiago cheese	1/3 cup	75 mL
Lemon juice	2 tsp.	10 mL

Chopped fresh rosemary, for garnish

Bring broth and rosemary to a boil in medium saucepan. Reduce heat to low. Cover to keep hot.

(continued on next page)

Melt butter in large saucepan on medium. Add rice. Heat and stir for about 1 minute until coated. Add 1 cup (250 mL) hot broth mixture, stirring constantly until broth is almost absorbed. Repeat with remaining broth mixture, 1 cup (250 mL) at a time, until broth is absorbed and rice is tender and creamy.

Add cheese and lemon juice. Stir.

Garnish with rosemary. Makes about 4 1/2 cups (1.1 L).

1/2 cup (125 mL): 160 Calories; 4.0 g Total Fat (0.5 g Mono, 0 g Poly, 2.5 g Sat); 10 mg Cholesterol; 26 g Carbohydrate; 0 g Fibre; 3 g Protein; 410 mg Sodium

Pictured on page 89.

Pesto Vegetable Braise

Braised vegetables, bright in both colour and flavour. Nothing but delicious!

Olive oil	2 tsp.	10 mL
Sliced fennel bulb (white part only)	1 cup	250 mL
Thinly sliced carrot, cut diagonally	1 cup	250 mL
Sliced onion	1/2 cup	125 mL
Prepared vegetable broth	1/2 cup	125 mL
Garlic clove, minced (or 1/4 tsp., 1 mL, powder)	1	1
Salt	1/8 tsp.	0.5 mL
Pepper	1/4 tsp.	1 mL
Sliced red pepper	2 cups	500 mL
Sliced green pepper	1 cup	250 mL
Sun-dried tomato pesto	2 tbsp.	30 mL

Heat olive oil in large frying pan on medium. Add next 3 ingredients. Cook for about 8 minutes, stirring often, until onion is softened.

Add next 4 ingredients. Stir. Bring to a boil. Cook, covered, for about 2 minutes until carrot is tender-crisp.

Add remaining 3 ingredients. Stir. Cook, uncovered, for about 5 minutes, stirring occasionally, until peppers are tender-crisp. Makes about 5 cups (1.25 L).

1/2 cup (125 mL): 35 Calories; 2.0 g Total Fat (0.5 g Mono, 0 g Poly, 0 g Sat); 0 mg Cholesterol; 5 g Carbohydrate; 1 g Fibre; trace Protein; 85 mg Sodium

Pictured on page 143.

Roasted Rosemary Potatoes

Rosemary is native to the Mediterranean region, and this recipe adds the popular herb to tender roast potatoes. A broadly appealing side dish.

Baby potatoes, halved	1 1/2 lbs.	680 g
Medium onion, cut into 8 wedges	1	1
Olive oil	2 tbsp.	30 mL
Garlic clove, sliced (or 1/4 tsp., 1 mL, powder)	1	1
Salt	1/2 tsp.	2 mL
Pepper	1/4 tsp.	1 mL
Chopped fresh rosemary	1 tsp.	5 mL

Toss first 6 ingredients in large bowl. Arrange in single layer on greased baking sheet with sides. Cook in 450°F (230°C) oven for about 30 minutes until potatoes are tender and starting to brown. Transfer to serving bowl.

Sprinkle with rosemary. Toss. Makes about 3 1/2 cups (875 mL).

1/2 cup (125 mL): 120 Calories; 4.0 g Total Fat (3.0 g Mono, 0 g Poly, 0.5 g Sat); 0 mg Cholesterol; 20 g Carbohydrate; 2 g Fibre; 3 g Protein; 140 mg Sodium

Pictured on page 54.

Italian Barley Pilaf

This colourful side dish is the perfect accompaniment for grilled or roasted meat or fish.

Water	6 cups	1.5 L
Pot barley	1 cup	250 mL
Olive oil	1 tbsp.	15 mL
Finely chopped carrot	1 cup	250 mL
Finely chopped onion	1 cup	250 mL
Finely chopped zucchini (with peel)	1 cup	250 mL
Dried oregano	1/2 tsp.	2 mL
Salt	1/2 tsp.	2 mL
Pepper	1/8 tsp.	0.5 mL

(continued on next page)

Sides

Diced seeded tomato	1 cup	250 mL
Chopped fresh basil	2 tbsp.	30 mL
White wine vinegar	1 tsp.	5 mL

Bring water to a boil in large saucepan. Add barley. Stir. Boil, uncovered, for about 30 minutes, stirring occasionally, until tender. Drain. Return to same pot. Cover to keep warm.

Heat olive oil in large frying pan on medium. Add next 6 ingredients. Cook for about 10 minutes, stirring often, until vegetables are softened.

Add remaining 3 ingredients and barley. Stir. Makes about 5 1/2 cups (1.4 L).

1/2 cup (125 mL): 80 Calories; 1.5 g Total Fat (1.0 g Mono, 0 g Poly, 0 g Sat); 0 mg Cholesterol; 16 g Carbohydrate; 3 g Fibre; 2 g Protein; 95 mg Sodium

Pictured on page 143.

Herbed Beans and Pine Nuts

Bright green beans add cheer to any meal, with pine nuts adding a nice crunch.

Butter (or hard margarine)	1 tbsp.	15 mL
Pine nuts	2 tbsp.	30 mL
Fresh (or frozen) whole green beans	4 cups	1 L
Chopped fresh parsley	1 tsp.	5 mL
Chopped fresh rosemary	1/2 tsp.	2 mL
Chopped fresh thyme	1/2 tsp.	2 mL
Salt	1/4 tsp.	1 mL
Pepper, sprinkle		

Melt butter in small frying pan on medium. Add pine nuts. Heat and stir for about 1 minute until butter starts to brown and nuts are golden. Set aside.

Pour water into large saucepan until 1 inch (2.5 cm) deep. Bring to a boil. Add green beans. Stir. Reduce heat to medium. Boil gently, covered, for about 5 minutes until tender-crisp. Drain. Transfer to medium bowl.

Add remaining 5 ingredients and pine nut mixture. Toss. Makes about 3 1/2 cups (875 mL).

1/2 cup (125 mL): 40 Calories; 3.5 g Total Fat (1.0 g Mono, 1.0 g Poly, 1.0 g Sat); trace Cholesterol; 3 g Carbohydrate; 1 g Fibre; trace Protein; 85 mg Sodium

Pictured on page 143.

Sides

Orange Ricotta Cheesecake

A cookie-like crust of almond shortbread hides beneath a decadent orange ricotta cheesecake. It's tough to determine what's the best part of this dessert. This one's a sure-fire favourite.

ALMOND SHORTBREAD CRUST

Butter (or hard margarine), softened	1/2 cup	125 mL
Granulated sugar	2 tbsp.	30 mL
All-purpose flour	1 cup	250 mL
Ground almonds	1/2 cup	125 mL

FILLING

Large eggs	3	3
Ricotta cheese	4 cups	1 L
Liquid honey	3/4 cup	175 mL
All-purpose flour	3 tbsp.	50 mL
Grated orange zest	1 tbsp.	15 mL
Salt	1/8 tsp.	0.5 mL
Sliced natural almonds	1/4 cup	60 mL

Almond Shortbread Crust: Beat butter and sugar in medium bowl until light and creamy. Add flour and ground almonds. Stir until no dry flour remains. Press into bottom of ungreased 9 inch (23 cm) springform pan. Bake in 350°F (175°C) oven for about 25 minutes until golden. Let stand until cool.

Filling: Beat first 6 ingredients in large bowl until just combined. Spread evenly over crust. Bake in 350°F (175°C) oven for 30 minutes.

Scatter sliced almonds over top. Bake for about 40 minutes until set along edges but centre still wobbles. Run knife around inside edge of pan to allow cheesecake to settle evenly. Let stand in pan on wire rack until cooled completely. Chill, covered, for at least 6 hours or overnight. Cuts into 12 wedges.

1 wedge: 340 Calories; 18.0 g Total Fat (6.0 g Mono, 1.5 g Poly, 9.0 g Sat); 80 mg Cholesterol; 34 g Carbohydrate; 1 g Fibre; 13 g Protein; 190 mg Sodium

Fruit Pizza

With ricotta cheese, pistachios and fruit, what's not to love? This delightful dessert pizza was inspired by another Italian sweet—the cannoli. As an added perk, this dessert can easily be made a day in advance.

All-purpose flour	1 1/4 cups	300 mL
Coarsely chopped pistachios	1 cup	250 mL
Brown sugar, packed	1/3 cup	75 mL
Grated orange zest	1/2 tsp.	2 mL
Cold butter (or hard margarine), cut up	2/3 cup	150 mL
Block cream cheese, softened	4 oz.	125 g
Ricotta cheese	1/2 cup	125 mL
Granulated sugar	1/4 cup	60 mL
Vanilla extract	1/2 tsp.	2 mL
Cans of mandarin orange segments, drained (10 oz., 284 mL, each)	2	2
Halved red seedless grapes	1 cup	250 mL
Coarsely chopped pistachios	1 tbsp.	15 mL

Process first 4 ingredients in food processor until pistachios are finely chopped. Add butter. Process with on/off motion until mixture resembles coarse crumbs. Press evenly into greased 12 inch (30 cm) pizza pan. Bake in 350°F (175°C) oven for about 14 minutes until golden. Let stand on wire rack until cool.

Beat next 4 ingredients in medium bowl until smooth. Spread over crust, almost to edge.

Arrange oranges and grapes over cheese mixture.

Scatter second amount of pistachios over top. Cuts into 12 wedges.

1 wedge: 310 Calories; 19.0 g Total Fat (5.0 g Mono, 2.0 g Poly, 9.0 g Sat); 40 mg Cholesterol; 31 g Carbohydrate; 2 g Fibre; 6 g Protein; 115 mg Sodium

Sweet Basil Panna Cotta

Certainly a unique dessert, with a mild basil flavour coming through as a pleasant surprise. Sweet, delicious and elegant.

Envelope of unflavoured gelatin (about 2 1/4 tsp., 11 mL)	1/4 oz.	7 g
Milk	1/2 cup	125 mL
Whipping cream	1 cup	250 mL
Milk	3/4 cup	175 mL
Granulated sugar	1/2 cup	125 mL
Vanilla extract	1 tsp.	5 mL
Basil leaves	3	3

Sprinkle gelatin over first amount of milk in small bowl. Let stand for 1 minute.

Combine remaining 5 ingredients in medium saucepan. Bring to a boil on medium, stirring occasionally. Remove from heat. Remove and discard basil leaves. Add gelatin mixture. Stir until dissolved. Pour through fine sieve into liquid measure. Discard solids. Pour into 6 greased 1/2 cup (125 mL) ramekins. Chill, covered, for at least 6 hours or overnight until set. Makes 6 panna cotta.

1 panna cotta: 210 Calories; 13.0 g Total Fat (3.5 g Mono, 0 g Poly, 3.0 g Sat); 50 mg Cholesterol; 22 g Carbohydrate; 0 g Fibre; 3 g Protein; 50 mg Sodium

Fruit Zabaglione

Zabaglione (pronounced zah-bahl-YOH-nay) is a warm, creamy custard typically made from egg yolks, wine and sugar. This mildly cinnamon-spiced version is guaranteed to live up to all expectations.

Can of sliced peaches in juice, drained	14 oz.	398 mL
Halved red seedless grapes	1 cup	250 mL
Medium orange, segmented (see Tip, page 141)	1	1
Egg yolks (large)	4	4
Marsala wine	1/2 cup	125 mL
Granulated sugar	1/4 cup	60 mL
Ground cinnamon, sprinkle		

(continued on next page)

Sweets

Divide first 3 ingredients into 4 serving bowls.

Whisk remaining 4 ingredients in medium heatproof bowl. Set bowl over simmering water in large saucepan so that bottom of bowl is not touching water. Cook for about 7 minutes, whisking constantly, until foamy and thickened. Spoon over fruit. Serves 4.

1 serving: 240 Calories; 4.5 g Total Fat (2.0 g Mono, 0.5 g Poly, 1.5 g Sat); 210 mg Cholesterol; 40 g Carbohydrate; 2 g Fibre; 4 g Protein; 25 mg Sodium

Variation: For an alcohol-free alternative, use the juice from the canned peaches in place of Marsala wine.

Minty Melon Sorbetto

Whether you call it sorbet, sherbet or sorbetto (as the Italians do), this refreshing dessert is the perfect ending to a meal on a hot summer's day. Choose ripe cantaloupe for best flavour.

Granulated sugar	1/2 cup	125 mL
Fresh mint leaves, lightly packed	1/4 cup	60 mL
Lemon juice	1/4 cup	60 mL
Water	1/4 cup	60 mL
Chopped cantaloupe	3 cups	750 mL

Heat and stir first 4 ingredients in small saucepan on medium until sugar is dissolved. Bring to a boil. Reduce heat to medium-low. Simmer, covered, for 5 minutes. Strain through sieve into medium bowl. Discard solids.

Process cantaloupe in blender or food processor until smooth. Add to sugar mixture. Stir. Pour into ungreased 9 x 13 inch (23 x 33 cm) pan. Freeze, covered, for 1 hour. Scrape and stir to break up ice crystals. Repeat every hour for 3 hours until set. Scoop into small bowls to serve. Makes about 3 3/4 cups (925 mL).

1/3 cup (75 mL): 45 Calories; 0 g Total Fat (0 g Mono, 0 g Poly, 0 g Sat); 0 mg Cholesterol; 12 g Carbohydrate; 0 g Fibre; 0 g Protein; 5 mg Sodium

 tip To segment citrus, trim a small slice of peel from both ends so the flesh is exposed. Place the fruit, bottom cut-side down, on a cutting board. Remove the peel with a sharp knife, cutting down and around the flesh, leaving as little pith as possible. Over a small bowl, cut on either side of the membranes to release the segments.

Lemon Cherry Tarts

These versatile tarts combine a few simple ingredients for an easy dessert that's somewhat reminiscent of cheesecake. Make them a day in advance and store in the fridge, or freeze them for up to 4 weeks.

Unsweetened tart shells	18	18
Whipping cream	1/2 cup	125 mL
Granulated sugar	1/3 cup	75 mL
Mascarpone cheese	1 cup	250 mL
Grated lemon zest	1 tsp.	5 mL
Pitted sour cherries, drained well and chopped	1 cup	250 mL

Arrange tart shells on ungreased baking sheet with sides. Bake in 375°F (190°C) oven for about 15 minutes until golden. Cool.

Beat whipping cream and sugar in small bowl until stiff peaks form.

Using same beaters, beat cheese and lemon zest in medium bowl until smooth.

Fold in cherries and whipped cream mixture. Spoon into tart shells. Makes 18 tarts.

1 tart: 200 Calories; 14.0 g Total Fat (4.0 g Mono, 2.0 g Poly, 6.0 g Sat); 20 mg Cholesterol; 17 g Carbohydrate; trace Fibre; 2 g Protein; 150 mg Sodium

1. Pesto Vegetable Braise, page 135
2. Herbed Beans and Pine Nuts, page 137
3. Italian Barley Pilaf, page 136

Props: Casa Bugatti

Rosemary Lemon Cookies

These outstanding cookies have a cake-like texture. Great with a cup of tea, or just for a snack. Makes a big enough batch that you can freeze some.

Butter (or hard margarine), softened	1/2 cup	125 mL
Granulated sugar	1 cup	250 mL
Large egg	1	1
Ricotta cheese	1 cup	250 mL
Lemon juice	2 tbsp.	30 mL
Chopped fresh rosemary	1 tbsp.	15 mL
Grated lemon zest (see Tip, page 94)	2 tsp.	10 mL
All-purpose flour	2 cups	500 mL
Baking soda	1/2 tsp.	2 mL
Salt	1/2 tsp.	2 mL

Beat butter and sugar in large bowl until light and fluffy.

Add next 5 ingredients. Beat well.

Combine remaining 3 ingredients in small bowl. Add to sugar mixture in 2 additions, mixing well after each addition, until no dry flour remains. Drop, using 1 tbsp. (15 mL) for each, about 1 inch (2.5 cm) apart, onto greased cookie sheets. Bake in 350°F (175°C) oven for about 12 minutes until golden. Let stand on cookie sheets for 5 minutes before removing to wire racks to cool. Makes about 53 cookies.

1 cookie: 50 Calories; 2.0 g Total Fat (0.5 g Mono, 0 g Poly, 1.5 g Sat); 10 mg Cholesterol; 8 g Carbohydrate; 0 g Fibre; 1 g Protein; 50 mg Sodium

Pictured at left.

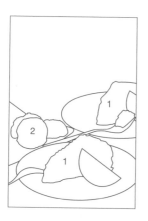

1. Citrus Polenta Cake, page 147
2. Rosemary Lemon Cookies, above

Tiramisu

Rich, creamy and decadent. It's hard to find a better dessert than tiramisu. If you'd rather make this an alcohol-free dessert, increase the amount of coffee to replace the Marsala wine. Fresh raspberries make a nice, colourful garnish.

Whipping cream	1 cup	250 mL
Mascarpone cheese	2 cups	500 mL
Granulated sugar	1/3 cup	75 mL
Marsala wine	1 tbsp.	15 mL
Cold strong prepared coffee	1/2 cup	125 mL
Marsala wine	3 tbsp.	50 mL
Granulated sugar	2 tbsp.	30 mL
Ladyfingers, approximately	24	24
Cocoa	1 tbsp.	15 mL

Beat whipping cream in small bowl until soft peaks form.

Using same beaters, beat next 3 ingredients in medium bowl until smooth. Fold in whipped cream.

Stir next 3 ingredients in small shallow bowl until sugar is dissolved. Quickly dip half of ladyfingers into coffee mixture, 1 at a time, until partially soaked through. Arrange in single layer in ungreased 8 x 8 inch (20 x 20 cm) baking dish, trimming to fit if necessary. Spread half of cheese mixture evenly over ladyfingers. Repeat with remaining ladyfingers, coffee mixture and cheese mixture.

Sift cocoa through fine sieve over top. Chill, covered, for at least 4 hours or overnight. Cuts into 9 pieces.

1 piece: 380 Calories; 28.0 g Total Fat (4.5 g Mono, 0.5 g Poly, 17.0 g Sat); 165 mg Cholesterol; 26 g Carbohydrate; 0 g Fibre; 6 g Protein; 170 mg Sodium

 Tiramisu is often thought of as the Italian equivalent of the English trifle. The word *tiramisu* literally translates to "carry me up," which is certainly fitting for a dessert as heavenly as this.

Citrus Polenta Cake

To further add to the sophistication, brush this lovely cake with orange-flavoured liqueur while it's still warm, add a sprinkle of icing sugar, or garnish with orange wedges. This can also be made into a gluten-free recipe by using gluten-free baking powder.

Ground almonds	1 1/2 cups	375 mL
Yellow cornmeal	1 cup	250 mL
Baking powder	2 tsp.	10 mL
Baking soda	1/2 tsp.	2 mL
Salt	1/4 tsp.	1 mL
Large eggs	2	2
Buttermilk (or soured milk, see Tip, page 42)	1 1/4 cups	300 mL
Granulated sugar	2/3 cup	150 mL
Olive (or cooking) oil	1/3 cup	75 mL
Lemon juice	2 tbsp.	30 mL
Orange juice	2 tbsp.	30 mL
Grated lemon zest (see Tip, page 94)	1 tsp.	5 mL
Grated orange zest (see Tip, page 94)	1 tsp.	5 mL

Combine first 5 ingredients in large bowl.

Beat remaining 8 ingredients in medium bowl. Add to cornmeal mixture. Beat well. Pour into greased 9 inch (23 cm) springform pan. Bake in 350°F (175°C) oven for about 35 minutes until wooden pick inserted in centre of cake comes out clean. Let stand on wire rack until cool. Cuts into 12 wedges.

1 wedge: 240 Calories; 13.0 g Total Fat (9.0 g Mono, 2.5 g Poly, 1.5 g Sat); 25 mg Cholesterol; 26 g Carbohydrate; 2 g Fibre; 5 g Protein; 160 mg Sodium

Pictured on page 144.

Strawberry Marsala Spumoni

Spumoni (pronounced spoo-MOH-nee) is an Italian ice cream dessert, usually consisting of various flavours that have been layered in a mold. This version includes Marsala wine for added interest.

Marsala wine	1/4 cup	60 mL
Chopped dried cherries	2 tbsp.	30 mL
Strawberry ice cream, softened	3 cups	750 mL
Whipping cream	1 cup	250 mL
Icing (confectioner's) sugar	3 tbsp.	50 mL
Flaked hazelnuts (filberts), toasted (see Tip, page 46)	2 tbsp.	30 mL
Minced crystallized ginger	2 tbsp.	30 mL
Chocolate ice cream, softened	3 cups	750 mL

Stir wine and cherries in small bowl. Set aside.

Spread strawberry ice cream evenly in plastic wrap-lined 9 x 5 x 3 inch (23 x 12.5 x 7.5 cm) loaf pan. Freeze for 30 minutes.

Beat whipping cream and icing sugar in medium bowl until stiff peaks form.

Fold in hazelnuts, ginger and cherry mixture. Spread evenly over strawberry ice cream. Freeze for about 1 hour until firm.

Spread chocolate ice cream over whipped cream mixture. Freeze, covered, for at least 6 hours or overnight. Invert onto cutting board. Discard plastic wrap. Cuts into 12 slices.

1 slice: 220 Calories; 14.0 g Total Fat (3.5 g Mono, 0 g Poly, 8.0 g Sat); 45 mg Cholesterol; 23 g Carbohydrate; trace Fibre; 3 g Protein; 55 mg Sodium

Variation: Use the same amount of white grape juice in place of Marsala wine.

Chocolate Fig Biscotti

Biscotti and coffee make great companions for one another. So why not enjoy a piece of this crispy biscotti at your mid-morning coffee break? Figs and chocolate chips go surprisingly well together.

All-purpose flour	2 1/4 cups	550 mL
Cocoa, sifted if lumpy	1/2 cup	125 mL
Baking soda	1 tsp.	5 mL
Salt	3/4 tsp.	4 mL
Butter (or hard margarine), softened	1/3 cup	75 mL
Brown sugar, packed	3/4 cup	175 mL
Large eggs	2	2
Liquid honey	1/4 cup	60 mL
Vanilla extract	1 tsp.	5 mL
Chopped dried figs	1/2 cup	125 mL
Mini semi-sweet chocolate chips	1/2 cup	125 mL

Combine first 4 ingredients in medium bowl.

Beat butter and sugar in large bowl until light and fluffy. Add next 3 ingredients. Beat well. Add flour mixture in 2 additions, beating well after each addition until no dry flour remains.

Add figs and chocolate chips. Mix well. Divide dough into 2 equal portions. Roll each portion into 8 inch (20 cm) long log. Place about 3 inches (7.5 cm) apart on greased cookie sheet. Flatten logs slightly. Bake in 350°F (175°C) oven for about 25 minutes until edges are crisp. Let stand on cookie sheet for about 10 minutes until cool enough to handle. Transfer to cutting board. Using serrated knife, cut each log diagonally into 1/2 inch (12 mm) slices. Arrange on greased cookie sheets. Reduce heat to 275°F (140°C). Bake for about 10 minutes per side until dry and crisp. Let stand on cookie sheets for 5 minutes before removing to wire racks to cool. Makes about 28 biscotti.

1 biscotti: 120 Calories; 3.5 g Total Fat (1.0 g Mono, 0 g Poly, 2.0 g Sat); 15 mg Cholesterol; 21 g Carbohydrate; 1 g Fibre; 2 g Protein; 135 mg Sodium

Amaretti Tartufi

This version of tartufi, *the Italian word for truffles, is like a fusion of candy and truffles. With a lovely sweetness and great texture from almonds, these bite-sized treats offer pure satisfaction.*

Golden corn syrup	1/4 cup	60 mL
Smooth peanut butter	3 tbsp.	50 mL
Almond liqueur	1 tbsp.	15 mL
Finely crushed vanilla wafers (about 32 wafers)	1 cup	250 mL
Ground almonds	1/2 cup	125 mL
Icing (confectioner's) sugar	1/4 cup	60 mL

Combine first 3 ingredients in medium bowl.

Add wafer crumbs and almonds. Stir well. Roll into balls, using about 1 1/2 tsp. (7 mL) for each.

Roll balls in icing sugar until coated. Makes about 40 truffles.

1 truffle: 35 Calories; 2.0 g Total Fat (0.5 g Mono, 0 g Poly, 0 g Sat); 0 mg Cholesterol; 5 g Carbohydrate; 0 g Fibre; trace Protein; 15 mg Sodium

 fyi The chocolate truffle was named as such because it quite closely resembles the other truffle—a rare fungi—in appearance. These two culinary favourites share more of a connection than just their looks—both are popular in Italian cuisine.

Measurement Tables

Throughout this book measurements are given in Conventional and Metric measure. To compensate for differences between the two measurements due to rounding, a full metric measure is not always used. The cup used is the standard 8 fluid ounce. Temperature is given in degrees Fahrenheit and Celsius. Baking pan measurements are in inches and centimetres as well as quarts and litres. An exact metric conversion is given below as well as the working equivalent (Metric Standard Measure).

Spoons

Conventional Measure	Metric Exact Conversion Millilitre (mL)	Metric Standard Measure Millilitre (mL)
1/8 teaspoon (tsp.)	0.6 mL	0.5 mL
1/4 teaspoon (tsp.)	1.2 mL	1 mL
1/2 teaspoon (tsp.)	2.4 mL	2 mL
1 teaspoon (tsp.)	4.7 mL	5 mL
2 teaspoons (tsp.)	9.4 mL	10 mL
1 tablespoon (tbsp.)	14.2 mL	15 mL

Cups

Conventional Measure	Metric Exact Conversion Millilitre (mL)	Metric Standard Measure Millilitre (mL)
1/4 cup (4 tbsp.)	56.8 mL	60 mL
1/3 cup (5 1/3 tbsp.)	75.6 mL	75 mL
1/2 cup (8 tbsp.)	113.7 mL	125 mL
2/3 cup (10 2/3 tbsp.)	151.2 mL	150 mL
3/4 cup (12 tbsp.)	170.5 mL	175 mL
1 cup (16 tbsp.)	227.3 mL	250 mL
4 1/2 cups	1022.9 mL	1000 mL (1 L)

Oven Temperatures

Fahrenheit (°F)	Celsius (°C)
175°	80°
200°	95°
225°	110°
250°	120°
275°	140°
300°	150°
325°	160°
350°	175°
375°	190°
400°	205°
425°	220°
450°	230°
475°	240°
500°	260°

Dry Measurements

Conventional Measure Ounces (oz.)	Metric Exact Conversion Grams (g)	Metric Standard Measure Grams (g)
1 oz.	28.3 g	28 g
2 oz.	56.7 g	57 g
3 oz.	85.0 g	85 g
4 oz.	113.4 g	125 g
5 oz.	141.7 g	140 g
6 oz.	170.1 g	170 g
7 oz.	198.4 g	200 g
8 oz.	226.8 g	250 g
16 oz.	453.6 g	500 g
32 oz.	907.2 g	1000 g (1 kg)

Pans

Conventional Inches	Metric Centimetres
8x8 inch	20x20 cm
9x9 inch	23x23 cm
9x13 inch	23x33 cm
10x15 inch	25x38 cm
11x17 inch	28x43 cm
8x2 inch round	20x5 cm
9x2 inch round	23x5 cm
10x4 1/2 inch tube	25x11 cm
8x4x3 inch loaf	20x10x7.5 cm
9x5x3 inch loaf	23x12.5x7.5 cm

Casseroles

CANADA & BRITAIN Standard Size Casserole	Exact Metric Measure	UNITED STATES Standard Size Casserole	Exact Metric Measure
1 qt. (5 cups)	1.13 L	1 qt. (4 cups)	900 mL
1 1/2 qts. (7 1/2 cups)	1.69 L	1 1/2 qts. (6 cups)	1.35 L
2 qts. (10 cups)	2.25 L	2 qts. (8 cups)	1.8 L
2 1/2 qts. (12 1/2 cups)	2.81 L	2 1/2 qts. (10 cups)	2.25 L
3 qts. (15 cups)	3.38 L	3 qts. (12 cups)	2.7 L
4 qts. (20 cups)	4.5 L	4 qts. (16 cups)	3.6 L
5 qts. (25 cups)	5.63 L	5 qts. (20 cups)	4.5 L

Recipe Index

153

W

Z

Cheddar Chili Tarts

Healthy Recipe Makeovers, Page 13

Whole-wheat flour tortillas are a great low-fat alternative to pastry in these tasty tarts.

Whole-wheat flour tortillas (10 inch, 25 cm, diameter)	4	4
Grated sharp Cheddar cheese	1/2 cup	125 mL
Large eggs	2	2
Milk	1/2 cup	125 mL
Dried crushed chilies	1/2 tsp.	2 mL
Pepper	1/4 tsp.	1 mL

Cut twelve 4 inch (10 cm) rounds from tortillas. Press rounds into greased muffin cups. Bake in 400°F (205°C) oven for about 8 minutes until golden and crisp. Let stand for 15 minutes. Reduce heat to 350°F (175°C).

Scatter cheese into tortilla cups.

Whisk remaining 4 ingredients in small bowl. Pour over cheese. Bake for about 20 minutes until puffed and set. Makes 12 tarts.

BEFORE: *1 tart: 179 Calories; 12.9 g Total Fat (6.6 g Sat); 179 mg Sodium*

AFTER: *1 tart: 59 Calories; 3 g Total Fat (1.5 g Mono, 0 g Poly, 1 g Sat); 25 mg Cholesterol; 5 g Carbohydrate; 1 g Fibre; 3 g Protein; 122 mg Sodium*